A STRAIGHTFORWARD GUIDE
TO
SMALL CLAIMS IN THE COUNTY COURT

PETER WHIMSTER

STRAIGHTFORWARD PUBLISHING

ACKNOWLEDGEMENTS

I would particularly like to thank Elizabeth Tarn (Barrister) for her invaluable help in compiling this book.

I would like to dedicate this second edition to the memory of my dear father WF Whimster

Straightforward Publishing Limited
38 Cromwell Road, London E17 9JN

© Peter Whimster
Second Edition 1997

All rights reserved. No part of this publication may be reproduced, in a retrieval system or transmitted by any means, electronic or mechanical, photocopying or otherwise, without the prior permission of the copyright owner.

British Library Cataloguing in Publication data. A catalogue record for this book is available from the British Library.

ISBN 1 8999 21 3

Printed by BPC Wheaton – Exeter
Cover design by Straightforward Graphics

Whilst every effort has been taken to ensure the information given in the book is accurate at the time the book was printed, the author and publishers recognise that information can become out of date. The book is therefore sold on condition that no responsibility for errors or omissions is assumed. The author and publishers cannot be held liable for any loss which is a result of the use of any information contained herein.

CONTENTS

Introduction	7
1. Types of Small Claim	11
2. Before Legal Action	23
3. An Overview of Procedure	27
4. Plaintiff – how to complete a summons form	35
5. Defendant – how to respond	49
6. Evidence	59
7. The Costs of Arbitration	67
8. Preparing for the Arbitration Hearing	75
9. Settling the Dispute	81
10. Representation	87
11. Arbitration and Judgment	89
12. Enforcement	95
13. If Judgment has been entered against you	107
Glossary	115
Appendix 1 : Particulars of Claim	120
Appendix 2 : Order 19 (Reference to Arbitration)	127

INTRODUCTION TO THIS GUIDE

This guide will outline the small claims procedure known as "arbitration". Except for a brief summary in chapter 1 it will not tell you about "the law" or "your rights". The aim of this guide is to tell you about the procedure by which you can bring or defend a small claim and how to enforce a judgment.

The small claims procedure is designed to be used and understood by the general public without legal representation in order to provide cost effective resolution of minor disputes. As a result the person who wins the case cannot normally recover their legal costs from their opponent. A small claim is one which involves a sum of money below £3,000. This limit has recently been increased from £1,000. Small claims are heard in local courts known as county courts.

The arbitrator who decides the case will be a district judge and in this guide these two terms are used interchangeably. The person who is bringing the claim to arbitration is called the "plaintiff" and the person he is making the claim against is known as the "defendant". When an arbitration hearing has taken place the arbitrator will reach a decision known as a "judgment". This is a court order which usually requires certain action. For example the defendant might be ordered to pay the plaintiff compensation which is known as "damages".

We very much hope that this guide will prove to be valuable to those who wish to pursue or defend a small claim, in the county courts.

A STRAIGHTFORWARD GUIDE TO SMALL CLAIMS

If you have any comments concerning the contents and information in this book please do not hesitate to contact Straightforward Publishing at: 38 Cromwell Road, Walthamstow, London E17 9JN.

FORMS

This guide contains county court forms printed by permission of the Lord Chancellor's Department. Although care has been taken to reproduce the correct forms, the forms printed are reproduced to illustrate and explain the text. Care should be taken to collect the right forms from the court office and to use the correct forms in pursuing your claim or defending a claim against you. *All such forms are Crown Copyright and they are reproduced with the kind permission of the Controller of HMSO.*

RULES OF THE COUNTY COURT

The procedure in this guide is derived from the Rules of the county Court Relating to Arbitration. The principal rule is Rule 19 which is printed in Appendix 2.

GENDER

For convenience, the masculine gender has been used throughout this book and is in no way intended to indicate bias or sexism.

Important Note: This guide applies to England & Wales. The law and procedure in Scotland & Northern Ireland is different and this guide should not be used in those countries.

1 TYPES OF 'SMALL CLAIM'

Most disputes which involve less than £3,000 and which are not exceptionally complex are automatically referred to small claims arbitration, however, a Small Claim will most likely result from a breach of contract. This includes non-payment of an invoice which has been properly issued. A claim for payment is a simple matter involving a claim for financial compensation.

THE SUPPLIERS RIGHT TO PAYMENT

Where goods are delivered or services rendered, the supplier or service provider is entitled to the agreed price or agreed payment for the service rendered. If no price has been agreed, the supplier or service provider is entitled to a reasonable sum for the goods supplied or service rendered.

THE PURCHASER'S RIGHTS

When goods are supplied which do not comply with the contract, or in breach of terms implied by the Sale of Goods Act (see below), the purchaser is entitled to either:–

- compensation known as "damages", or

- if the breach is serious, to reject the goods and claim damages for financial loss, for example, a refund of the purchase price, or the cost above the agreed purchase price for goods within the terms of the contract, and any additional loss suffered. The compensation claimed would be the purchase price and any other additional loss suffered. In this situation, the contract is discharged, which means that the purchaser is released of his obligation of payment, or

- to reject the goods and affirm the contract, which means that the contract is not discharged and the purchaser requires the supplier to perform the contract and holds the supplier to his contractual obligations. If the contract is not performed, the aggrieved party may sue for breach of contract.

SALE OF GOODS ACT, 1979

The Sale of Goods Act implies certain terms into contracts for the sale of goods. This means that the seller must supply goods which satisfy certain statutory terms of contract imposed by Parliament. The principal implied terms are:–

- the vendor must own the goods or have the right to sell them;

- if the goods are sold by description they must correspond with that description. This applies to goods which are described in some way by a label or a notice identifying the kind of goods they are, or to specific goods which the buyer has not seen at the time of the contract and which are bought on the basis of a description;

- where a seller sells goods in the course of a business the goods must be of satisfactory quality. This is defined as meaning that they must meet the standard that a reasonable person would regard as satisfactory, taking account of any description of the goods, the price (if relevant) and all the other relevant circumstances. The Act lists the following as aspects of the quality of goods; the fitness for the purpose for which goods of the kind in questions are commonly supplied, the appearance and finish, freedom from minor defects, safety and durability. These provisions do not apply to goods of unsatisfactory quality if the fault has been specifically drawn to the buyer's attention before the contract is made;

- if the goods are sold by sample the bulk must correspond to the sample in quality and be free from any defect which would not be apparent on reasonable examination of the sample.

If these conditions are not satisfied, the purchaser has the rights specified above, to damages, to rejection and damages, or to affirm the contract and claim damages for loss suffered.

SUPPLY OF GOODS AND SERVICES ACT, 1982

This Act relates to the supply of services which includes a vast range of activities, from having your house altered or redecorated, to having your hair dyed, to having your coat dry cleaned. It includes the supply of goods because often when services are supplied the materials required are also supplied such as paint for decorating, and these materials must be of a suitable standard.

The supplier of services is entitled to payment of his invoice and if a price has not been agreed he is entitled to a reasonable charge. Even if the work is not of a reasonable standard the supplier may be entitled to a reasonable payment.

Where a service is supplied by someone acting in the course of a business then purchaser is entitled to receive a service performed with reasonable care and skill and carried out within a reasonable time. If goods are supplied they must be of satisfactory quality and correspond to any description or sample by which they have been sold. If the work or goods are not of a reasonable standard the purchaser must prove that this is the case and may claim the remedies mentioned above. For example a purchaser may be entitled to damages if the work is so sub-standard that financial loss is suffered such as for plumbing or re-wiring which needs to be completely redone or a coat which needs to be replaced after cleaning. The Supply of Goods and Services Act also applies to contracts for the hire of goods although not to hire purchase agreements. Like contracts for sale, contracts for hire have terms implied into them that the supplier of the goods (the bailor) has the right to hire them out, that they correspond to any description or sample by reference to which the contract has been made and that where the goods are supplied in the course of business they will be of satisfactory quality. In addition, there is an implied term that the person who hires the goods (the bailee) will enjoy quiet possession of the goods for the agreed period unless they are taken by the owner or another person with a right or charge over them which the bailee was told or knew about before the contract was made.

QUANTUM MERUIT

This is a legal rule which is derived from previous cases rather than the supply of goods and services statute. It translates as "as much as he deserves" and means that if one party is prevented by the other, in breach of the contract, from completing the work he had contracted to perform then he may claim payment for what he has already done on a quantum meruit basis. A claim can also be made where partial performance has been voluntarily accepted by the other party.

The Cheque Rule

If goods or services are paid for by a cheque which is subsequently dishonoured the recipient can base his claim on the cheque and does not have to prove the contract which led to its payment. This is because the cheques, bills of exchange and promissory notes are regarded as independent contracts, separate from the contract for sale. Consequently there are only a few grounds on which a defendant can defend such a claim such of fraud, duress, total failure of consideration and possibly misrepresentation.

UNFAIR CONTRACT TERMS ACT, 1977

Contracts often include exclusion clauses, where one side attempts to limit its liability or the rights of the other party in the event of a breach of contract. The Unfair Contract Terms Act makes any clause excluding or limiting liability for death or personal injury void. Any exclusion clause which restricts or limits the terms implied by the Sale of Goods Act, where one party is dealing as a consumer, is void. This means that the exclusion has no effect. Any exclusion clause where one party is dealing on standard terms or one party is a business, will only be effective in so far as the person relying on it can prove that it is "reasonable" as defined by the Act which means that the term "shall have been a fair and reasonable one to be included having regard to the circumstances which were, or ought reasonably to have been known to or in the contemplation of the parties when the contract was made". It is for the person alleging that a term or notice is reasonable to show that it is.

PERSONAL INJURIES

Personal injury claims are treated differently to other claims in that they are not automatically referred to arbitration if the damages claimed exceed £1,000. This is because personal injury cases often raise difficult issues and the parties are more likely to need legal advice and representation the cost of which is not recoverable in small claims.

There has been some doubt about whether the £1,000 limit relates just to damages you are claiming for the physical injury itself or whether additional claims for things such as loss of earnings or the cost of treatment can be used to bring the claim over the arbitration limit. It seems that the £1,000 limit relates to the claim as a whole including the additional damages so for example if you claim £700 for the physical injury and £400 for physiotherapy, and loss of earnings, then your case would not be heard as a small claim. However you should consult the court staff about this point before beginning your case.

Personal injuries can have been caused deliberately but in most cases the Plaintiff seeks to prove that the defendant was negligent. Four points must be proved to establish negligence:

- that the defendant owed a duty of care. With regard to personal injuries everyone should take reasonable care to avoid doing things or failing to do things which they can reasonably foresee would be likely to injure people who they ought reasonably to have foreseen as being so affected by their acts or omissions;

- the defendant acted in breach of his duty;

    the breach caused the plaintiff's injury; and

- the injury was reasonably foreseeable, and not a "freak" accident";

- if the plaintiff was also negligent the court may find that he was guilty of contributing negligence and reduce the damages he receives to reflect the extent to which he was responsible;

- for causing his own injuries.

In the case of injury at work, the plaintiff could also claim compensation on the grounds that the defendant acted in breach of a

1 TYPES OF SMALL CLAIM

statutory duty, of which there are many imposed by the Health & Safety At Work legislation.

These areas are complicated and research should be undertaken before taking legal action. However, in legal terms, a simple case could well be suited to the small claims procedure.

CONSUMER PROTECTION ACT, 1987

This Act allows action against a "producer" of goods which are unsafe and cause personal injury or loss of or damage to property provided the value of the claim is over £275, excluding interest. The term producer includes the manufacturer, anyone who holds himself out as the producer by putting his name or trade mark on the product and an importer of the product into a Member State of the European Community from a place outside the EC in order to supply it to another in the course of his business. The Act does not apply to damage to the defective product itself or damage to any product supplied with a defective component comprised in it. Furthermore, there is no liability unless the product is a type of property ordinarily intended for private use, occupation or consumption and was intended by the Plaintiff mainly for such purposes. A person who suffers damage to his business property must therefore sue on a contract or in negligence.

THE OCCUPIER'S LIABILITY ACTS, 1957 AND 1984

The 1957 Act governs the liability of an occupier in respect of personal injury or damage to property suffered by those who come lawfully onto his premises as visitors. An occupier is under a duty to take such care as in all circumstances of the case is reasonable, to see that the visitor will be reasonably safe in using the premises for the purpose for which he is invited or is permitted to be there. An occupier can discharge his duty by warning his visitor of the particular danger provided that the warning is sufficient to enable the visitor to be reasonably safe.

The 1984 Act concerns the liability of an occupier with regard to people other than his visitors in respect of injuries suffered on the premises due to the state of the premises or things done or omitted to be done on them. This includes trespassers and people exercising private rights of way but not those using public rights of way. The occupier owes such people a duty if he is aware of a danger or has reasonable grounds to believe one exists, if he knows or has reasonable grounds to believe that the non-visitor is in the vicinity of the danger concerned or that he may come into the vicinity and the risk is one against which in all the circumstances of the case he may reasonably be expected to offer the non-visitor some protection. An occupier may be able to discharge his duty by taking reasonable steps to warn people of the danger but whether the warning is adequate will depend on the circumstances.

Housing Matters and Nuisance

This includes a wide variety of things many but not all of which are based on breach of contract. Examples include non payment of rent, failure to return a deposit, housing disrepair, illegal eviction, nuisance from noisy neighbours, harassment and so on. In this area rather than just seeking damages people may wish to apply for an injunction or an order for specific performance. This is where a court orders a person to do something or to refrain from doing something. For example, to repair a house or to refrain from disturbing their neighbours or to comply with the terms of an agreement. Up to £260 may be awarded for legal advice obtained in order to bring or defend a small claim for either an injunction or specific performance or similar relief but this does not cover the cost of being represented at the hearing.

1 TYPES OF SMALL CLAIM

Limitation Periods

The law imposes time limits, known as limitation periods within which you must commence your case. Time begins to run from the date of the breach of contract or the date of the actionable tort. Tort includes claims for negligence which are not based on breach of contract, nuisance and occupiers liability. In personal injury cases it runs from the date when the injury was sustained or, if it is later from the date when the plaintiff first knew of their injuries. The court has a discretion to extend the time available in personal injury cases in certain circumstances.

The time limits are:
Contract	3 years
Tort	6 years
Defective products (Consumer Protection Act 1987)	3 years
Personal injury	3 years

If you are the Defendant and the Plaintiff's claim is out of time you will have a defence to the claim but it is important that you mention it on your defence form as it is not automatic.

THINGS WHICH ARE NOT SMALL CLAIMS

Claims for the possession of land cannot be dealt with under the small claims procedure.

Employment disputes such as claims for unfair dismissal and sexual or racial discrimination are dealt with by Industrial Tribunals.

Is it a Small Claim?

Because legal aid is not available for small claims and your costs are not normally recoverable if you win, there is an incentive for plaintiffs with claims near the upper limit to inflate their claims to over £3,000. However the court regards this as a misuse of process which justifies restricting a successful plaintiff's costs to those he would have recovered under the small claims procedure. In these circumstances the Plaintiff is likely to have incurred more costs than he would have done if he had brought the case as a small claim and will have to pay them himself even if he wins his case. The test the court applies is "could the Plaintiff reasonably expect to be awarded more than £3,000?".

If you are a defendant faced with what you regard as an inflated claim you should state in your defence that the claim cannot reasonably exceed £3,000 and should be automatically referred to arbitration.

Where a claim is referred for arbitration a district judge may order that it should not be treated as a small claim and there should be a trial in court instead if:
- the case raises a difficult question of law or a complex question of fact or
- fraud is alleged against any party or
- the parties agree that the case should be tried in court or
- it would not be reasonable for the case to proceed as a small claim having regard to its subject matter, the size of any counterclaim and the circumstances of the parties or the interests of any other person likely to be affected by the award.
-

The judge can do this on his own initiative or in response to an application by any party.

1 TYPES OF SMALL CLAIM

KEY POINTS

- Most small claims are for breach of contract
- Small claims for personal injury caused by negligence or breach of statutory duty can be undertaken but the law is complicated and advice should be taken.

2 BEFORE LEGAL ACTION

PREVENT CLAIMS ARISING – PRE-EMPTIVE ACTION

Obviously it is highly desirable to avoid litigation if at all possible and the best way to do this is to prevent claims arising.

If you are a consumer and intend to employ someone to perform a service obtain estimates beforehand outlining exactly what is to be done and how much it will cost. It is also wise to ask if the people you are doing business with belong to any professional or trade associations. Write and confirm all the details of the contract before the work begins.

If you run a business, consider the benefits of a credit reference agency to check the creditworthiness of new customers. Reports can be obtained on–line via a computer and modem, for example, from Prestel. Depending on the service you are buying, ensure that you have a written contract or that you use your standard terms of business in a sale or purchase.

If you run a business and encounter serious problems in paying your creditors, always negotiate terms of
payment and discuss your situation openly and honestly. Such action at an early stage often avoids legal proceedings being taken against you. Always keep your bank manager informed and up to date with your business affairs and avoid giving him unexpected surprises.

Ensure that you keep all relevant documents, such as a receipt for a payment, the contract guarantees, delivery note or any letters written. Also keep a copy of any advertisement you relied on in entering into a contract. If you speak to anyone on the telephone, make a record of the person's name and of what was said. A case often turns on the documentary evidence available at the arbitration hearing and relevant documents with which you may have use to prove a case to the satisfaction of a judge usually come into existence before of during a dispute.

STEPS YOU SHOULD TAKE BEFORE TAKING LEGAL ACTION

The small claims court should be viewed as a last resort. Before issuing a Summons, make a clear complaint and attempt to reach a compromise by contacting the defendant. If no compromise or settlement is achieved, before issuing a Summons, you should write to the defendant threatening legal action and stating the recompense you are demanding. This is known as a "letter before action". It is important to keep a copy of this and of all correspondence.

You may decide you would like to try and negotiate a compromise or make an offer of settlement. If so refer to the chapter on settling the dispute.

Considerations before taking someone to court
Before issuing a summons to enforce a debt or payment of an invoice, etc., consider whether the defendant is worth suing. If he or she is completely penniless, you may live a longer and more contented life if you decided not to take legal action. A credit reference agency will be able to give you some idea of the creditworthiness of a potential defendant or you can check the register of county court judgments.

SAMPLE LETTERS BEFORE ACTION

Dear Mr. Cooke,

My tenancy in your flat at [address] ended on [date] and I duly moved out on that date. However I have still not received the repayment of my deposit of £____ which under the terms of our lease agreement you should repay at the end of the tenancy. If I do not receive the money requested within fourteen days of receipt of this letter then I will have no option but to begin legal proceedings against you.

Yours sincerely,

J. Smith

Dear Mrs. Gibson,

The washing machine I purchased from you on [date] is not of satisfactory quality or fit for the purpose for which is was sold. It has torn a number of garments of a total value of £600. I have already visited your shop and made a complaint but I have received no response.

I wish to return the faulty machine, have the purchase price refunded and for you to pay me the cost of replacing my clothes. If I do not receive a satisfactory reply within fourteen days I will begin legal proceedings against you in the County Court.

Yours sincerely,

J. Smith

Now please read the **KEY POINTS** from Chapter 2.

KEY POINTS

- Take pre-emptive action in order to avoid recourse to Law

- Before issuing legal proceedings, make a complaint first

- If a dispute is inevitable, and cannot be solved by negotiation, keep copies of all relevant letters and documents

- Even if you have a strong case, make sure that the defendant is worth suing. In some cases, it may be easier to walk away

- Before issuing a summons, ensure that you know the legal ground for your claim. If you are unsure, obtain advice from a Citizens Advice Bureau, Law Centre, Trade Union, or contact the Consumers' Association, whose lawyers will give legal advice for a small monthly fee

- Always write a letter before action before issuing a summons

- The County Court provides standard forms for issuing proceedings and the court staff will advise on procedure but cannot offer legal advice

3 AN OVERVIEW OF PROCEDURE

When a county court summons for £3,000 or less is issued, the dispute is categorised as a "small claim" and is automatically referred by the Court to "Arbitration". This in an informal procedure where a Judge hears each side of a dispute in a private room, rather than in an Open Court. Solicitors fees are not awarded to the successful party to an automatic Arbitration – unlike a hearing in Open Court. This is to encourage members of the public to conduct their own case.

The Court provides standard forms for completion by the opponents throughout a case with the intention that for simple matters, you could present your own case.

The remainder of this guide is concerned with the steps to follow to conduct an arbitration without legal representation. Clearly, you might be in a stronger position and feel more confident if you employed a Solicitor to present your case, but be aware that if you win, you will not be entitled to recover your legal costs. The small claims procedure is designed for self-representation.

The steps you must take to begin a County Court action against another person(s) are as follows:

ISSUE A SUMMONS

A summons is a document which is used to start proceedings in the County Court. In small claims cases it is a form which the Plaintiff fills in. The next Chapter will tell you in detail how to do this. A summons form can be obtained from the Court Office. When you have completed the form two copies of the Summons must be taken to the Court Office and the Court Fee paid (see appendix 1). The court will then serve (i.e. post) the Summons on the Defendant with three forms, a Form of Admission (N9A), a form for filing a Defence (N9B) and a form for filing a Counterclaim (N9B). The Court will also:

- post a form called a "Plaint Note" (N205A) to you. This form records the details of the claim, the case number and date of service. The case number is now the reference point for your case and no steps can be taken without quoting it

- you will also receive a Request for Judgment which is attached to the Plaint Note. To claim damages two types of Summons are available, they are:

- a Summons claiming a fixed sum of money, known as a "liquidated demand" – Form N1, or

- a Summons claiming damages to be assessed, where the court must assess and determine the level of compensation payable – Form N2.

Court Service

The court will post the Summons to the Defendant with a Form of Admission, Defence and Counterclaim.

The Summons used in small claims is described as a "Default Summons". This is a summons used to start a "default action". The significance of the term "default" is that, if the Defendant does not file a defence, the court will order judgment in the Plaintiff's favour without a hearing. In other words, by issuing a default summons, the Defendant is summonsed to answer the Plaintiff's claim and if he fails to do so by not filing a defence, the court will order judgment for the Plaintiff. In the case of a claim for a fixed amount, the court will order payment of that amount. If the amount is not specified, the court will order judgment for the Plaintiff with damages to be assessed. A hearing date will be set for the assessment of damages.

FORMS OF ADMISSION

Defence and Counterclaim (Forms N9A and N9B)

The Defendant must return the Form of Admission (N9A), Defence and Counterclaim (N9B) to the Court within 14 days of the date of service printed on the summons. The Defendant has the following options:

Admission or Partial Admission

The Defendant may admit the whole claim by posting the Form of Admission direct to the Plaintiff. He can also make a request for time to pay. The Plaintiff must then either accept or reject the request returning the Form of Admission to the court office with the Request for Judgment. The Court will enter judgment but if the suggested method of payment is rejected, the Court will enter judgment and set a date for a hearing to consider the method of payment.

If the Defendant admits part of the claim, and the Plaintiff does not accept the sum offered, the offer may be rejected and the Defendant must file a defence in respect of the balance. The court will set a date for an arbitration hearing.

Defence

If the Defendant files a Defence, the Plaintiff will receive a copy from the Court and the case will be transferred to the Defendant's local court which will set a date for the Arbitration Hearing. If you are a Plaintiff and you expect the Defendant to file a defence, you will save time if you issue your Summons in his local County Court. If a Defence is not filed within 14 days of service, the Plaintiff may return the Request for Judgment, and Judgment–in–Default will be entered in his favour. He will then receive a copy of the Judgment which will be in the form of an order for immediate payment or payment by instalments. This may be set aside on certain grounds which are discussed further on in this book.

Counterclaim

The Defendant's counterclaim is a claim made by the Defendant against the Plaintiff which may be less than his claim, so his claim is reduced, or it may be greater. A counterclaim is a separate action. Rather than the Defendant issuing his own Summons, the dispute is managed in one set of proceedings by the defendant issuing a counterclaim. The Plaintiff is entitled to file a defence to the counterclaim. However, the Plaintiff is treated as having denied the allegations made in a counterclaim if a defence is not filed. Judgment–in–default is therefore not applicable to a counterclaim.

Date of the Arbitration Hearing

If a defence is filed, the court will set a date for the arbitration and issue directions – you will be notified by Form N18A. The Court must :
- give not less than 14 days notice of the date of the hearing, and
- issue directions before any hearing or pre– hearing.

Directions Issued by the Court

When you are notified of the date of the hearing, you will also receive directions, these are the courts instructions as to how the case should proceed. District Judges have wide powers to issue directions and local courts have their own practise. The purpose of directions is to ensure that the arbitration runs smoothly. The directions for an arbitration printed on Form N18A are usually limited to two:

- not less than 14 days before the date fixed for the hearing, each party must post to the other copies of any documents they intend to rely on at the hearing, and

- not less than 7 days before the hearing, a copy of any expert report on which each party intends to rely must be posted to both the court and the other party.

This process of exchanging documents is known as disclosure of evidence.

Enforcement Proceedings

If the Defendant does not comply with the Judgment, which is a Court Order, you will be entitled to take enforcement proceedings which are discussed further on in this book.

Now please read the **KEY POINTS** from chapter 3.

KEY POINTS

- The plaintiff must take the initiative and issue a default Summons. The plaintiff pursues the claim throughout. This includes obtaining judgment and, if the defendant does not observe the judgment, enforcement proceedings.

- The defendant's role is mainly reactive – but if there is no reaction, the plaintiff may be entitled to a default judgment.

- A default judgment can be set aside by the court.

4 THE PLAINTIFF - HOW TO COMPLETE A SUMMONS FORM

This chapter explains how to complete a summons form. Copies of the two summons forms are appended to this Chapter. Use Form N1 if you are claiming a fixed monetary sum (known as a liquidated demand) for example a debt, a dishonoured cheque, or to claim a refund for faulty goods. Use Form N2 in cases where the amount of money claimed needs to be assessed (known as unliquidated damages) for example in a personal injury claim.

THE PLAINTIFF'S NAME AND ADDRESS

The summons form requires the plaintiff's full name and address. If the plaintiff is a company give the address of the registered office. If it is a firm write "a firm" after the name. If you are an individual trading under another name write your name and then "trading as" and the name you use. If the plaintiff is under 18 he is a minor and so may bring an action for unpaid wages himself but for all other actions he must sue by a representative known as a "next friend" usually an adult relative or friend. In such cases Form number N235 is used.

Think carefully about whether the correct person is bringing the action. For example if a friend gave you some goods as a present which turn out to be faulty and you want a refund of the purchase price, then the person who actually bought the goods should be the one to bring the court action. This is because it is the purchaser who is a party to the contract which has been breached not the recipient of the gifts and only parties to the contract can sue for its breach. This rule is known as the doctrine of privity of contract.

Also consider whether you should be suing a company rather than the individual you dealt with. Was the individual merely acting as the representative of the company rather than dealing with you in their own right? If you have a consumer credit or hire purchase agreement you should usually act against the finance company rather than the retailer.

Part 2 is for if you want the court papers to be sent to you at a different address from the one given in Part 1. It is normally only completed if a solicitor is acting on your behalf.

THE DEFENDANT'S NAME AND ADDRESS

The defendant's full name and address should be given. If you do not know their full name write Mr. or Ms and give their surname and their initials if you know them. If it is a company, firm or using the trading name see the comments in relation to plaintiffs above. If the defendant is a company the address of its registered office will be on its headed notepaper or you can find it out by telephoning Companies House in Cardiff on 01222 380801.

If the defendant is a minor they will need to be represented in the case by someone known as their "guardian ad litem" usually a parent or other adult relative or friend. A summons should not be sent directly to the minor but instead should be sent to the parent or guardian or other adult who will be acting for them.

CATEGORY OF CLAIM

A brief description of what type of claim you are making is required in the next space. This means stating what the claim consists of for example, breach of contract, dishonoured cheque, non-payment of invoice or bad workmanship.

PARTICULARS OF CLAIM

The particulars or details of your claim must be set out in the largest box or on a separate piece of paper. It is important to use numbered paragraphs and to set out each point relevant to your case. For example in a contract claim you must state or "plead" the following:

- if it is relevant, say who the parties are;

- that there was a contract and when it was made, was it written or oral, can it be implied from letters and similar documents?

- the relevant terms of the contract including implied terms. For example terms implied by the Sale of Goods Act;

- that you have performed all or part of your side of the contract or why you have not done so;

- that the contract has been breached and give details of what the defendant has done or failed to do that puts him in breach;

- what damage you have suffered as a result of the defendants breach.

AND LASTLY, you must state what you claim; for example payment of an invoice (state the amount) and interest at the contractual or statutory rate.

If your claim is in tort rather than contract - for example you are saying that the defendant was negligent - then you must plead the following:

- who the parties are (if relevant);

- describe the accident or event which is the basis of your complaint and say when it took place;

- that the accident or act you are complaining about was caused by the defendant's negligence or breach of duty and give details;

- that you suffered damage as a result of the facts alleged and give details of all the damage.

AND LASTLY state what you are claiming by either giving a figure or saying that you would like the damages to be assessed. Claim interest.

You should then sign underneath the particulars.

WHAT TO DO NEXT

Take the two copies of the completed summons form to the court and pay the issue fee (see Appendix ...). Remember to keep a copy for yourself. The court may ask for copies. The court will stamp the summons form and post it to the defendant with forms of admission, defence and counterclaim, explained in the next chapter. The defendant must reply to your summons within 14 days from the date of service printed on the Plaint Note. A company has 16 days to reply.

If the Defendant files a defence, the court will post a copy to you. A form of Admission is returned direct to the Plaintiff.

OBTAINING JUDGMENT IN DEFAULT

Meanwhile, you will receive a Plaint Note from the Court with a Request for Judgment-in-Default attached (Form N18A). A copy is annexed to this chapter. If a defence is not filed (you will know because the court will inform you if one is received), complete and return the Request for Judgment to the court.

ACCEPTING AN ADMISSION AND OFFER OF PAYMENT

As explained in the next chapter, the court serves a summons on the defendant with a form of Admission Defence and Counterclaim. If the defendant admits the claim, the form of admission is posted direct to you, the plaintiff. You must then complete and return it to the court requesting judgment and an order for payment. You may request judgment but object to the method of payment, or accept a part admission but pursue the balance in respect of which the defendant should file a defence and/or counterclaim.

If the Defendant admits the claim but asks for time to pay, you may reject the proposal. In the event of a dispute, the court staff will set an amount with reference to the information supplied by the defendant. The order to pay is issued on form N30(2), but if you object to the level of instalments, you are entitled to make an application to the district judge using form N244 for him to set a level of instalments. the case is then transferred to the defendant's local court for a hearing.

Now please read the **KEY POINTS** from chapter 4.

A STRAIGHTFORWARD GUIDE TO SMALL CLAIMS

KEY POINTS

- When a Defence is filed, the case is transferred from the court where the summons was issued to the defendant's local court. If you expect the Defendant to file a Defence, you should consider issuing the Summons by posting it to the Defendants local court to avoid the time delay in the court transferring the case to that Court. Otherwise, a Default Summons may be issued in any County Court.

Forms Appended

I. Default summons – fixed amount (Form N1)
II. Default summons – unspecified amount (Form N2)
III. Notice of Issue of a Default Summons and Request for Judgment (Form N205A)
IV. Notice of Arbitration Hearing and Judge's Directions (Form N205A).

PLAINTIFF - HOW TO COMPLETE A SUMMONS FORM

County Court Summons

Case Number

In the

County Court

The court office is open from 10am to 4pm Monday to Friday

(1) Plaintiff's full name address

(2) Address for service (and) payment
(if not as above)
Ref/Tel no.

Telephone:

Seal

This summons is only valid if sealed by the court
If it is not sealed it should be sent to the court.

(3) Defendant's name address

What the plaintiff claims from you

Brief description of type of claim

Particulars of the plaintiff's claim against you

Amount claimed

Court fee

Solicitor's costs

Total amount

Summons issued on

What to do about this summons

You can
- **dispute the claim**
- **make a claim against the plaintiff**
- **admit the claim in full and offer to pay**
- **pay the total amount shown above**
- **admit only part of the claim**

For information on what to do or if you need further advice, please turn over.

Signed
Plaintiff('s solicitor)
(or see enclosed particulars of claim)

N1 Default summons (fixed amount) (Order 3, rule 3(2)(b))

Keep this summons, you may need to refer to it

A STRAIGHTFORWARD GUIDE TO SMALL CLAIMS

You have 21 days from the date of the postmark to reply to this summons
(A limited company served at its registered office has 16 days to reply.)

If you do nothing	Judgment may be entered against you without further notice.
If you dispute the claim	Complete the white defence form (N9B) and return it to the court office. The notes on the form explain what you should do.
If you want to make a claim against the plaintiff (counterclaim)	Complete boxes 5 and 6 on the white defence form (N9B) and return the form to the court office. The notes at box 5 explain what you should do.
If you admit all of the claim and you are asking for time to pay	Fill in the blue admission form (N9A). The notes on the form explain what you should do and where you should send the completed form.
If you admit all of the claim and you wish to pay now	Take or send the money to the person named at box (2) on the front of the summons. If there is no address in box (2), send the money to the address in box (1). Read How to Pay below.
If you admit only part of the claim	Fill in the white defence form (N9B) saying how much you admit, then either: Pay the amount admitted as explained in the box above; or Fill in the blue admission form (N9A) if you need time to pay

Interest on Judgments

If judgment is entered against you and is for more than £5000, the plaintiff may be entitled to interest on the total amount.

Registration of Judgments

If the summons results in a judgment against you, your name and address may be entered in the Register of County Court Judgments. This may make it difficult for you to get credit. A leaflet giving further information can be obtained from the court.

Further Advice

You can get help to complete the reply forms and information about court procedures at any county court office or citizens' advice bureau. The address and telephone number of your local court is listed under "Courts" in the phone book. When corresponding with the court, please address forms or letters to the Chief Clerk. Always quote the whole of the case number which appears at the top right corner on the front of this form; the court is unable to trace your case without it.

How to pay

- PAYMENT(S) MUST BE MADE to the person named at the address for payment quoting their reference and the court case number.
- DO NOT bring or send payments to the court. THEY WILL NOT BE ACCEPTED.
- You should allow at least 4 days for your payments to reach the plaintiff or his representative.
- Make sure that you keep records and can account for all payments made. Proof may be required if there is any disagreement. It is not safe to send cash unless you use registered post.
- A leaflet giving further advice about payment can be obtained from the court.
- If you need more information you should contact the plaintiff or his representative.

To be completed on the court copy only

Served on

By posting on

Officer

Marked "gone away" on

PLAINTIFF - HOW TO COMPLETE A SUMMONS FORM

County Court Summons

Case Number: *Always quote this*

In the _____ County Court

The court office is open from 10am to 4pm Monday to Friday

Telephone

Plaintiff's full name address

Plaintiff's Solicitor's address

Ref/Tel No.

Defendant's full name (including title e.g. Mr, Mrs or Miss) and address

seal

This summons is only valid if sealed by the court. If it is not sealed it should be sent to the court.

Keep this summons, you may need to refer to it.

What the plaintiff claims from you

Give brief description of type of claim

Particulars of the plaintiff's claim against you

Amount claimed	see particulars
Court fee	
Solicitor's costs	
Total Amount	

Summons issued on _____

What you should do

You have 21 days (16 days if you are a limited company served at your registered office) from the date of the postmark to either

- **defend the claim** by filling in the back of the enclosed form and **sending it to the court**;

  OR

- **admit the claim** and make an offer of payment, by filling in the front of the enclosed reply form and **sending it to the court**.

If **you do nothing** judgment may be entered against you.

Please read the information on the back of the form. It will tell you more about what to do.

My claim is worth £5000 or less ☐   over £5000 ☐
All cases over £1000
I would like my case decided by   trial ☐   arbitration ☐

Signed
Plaintiff or plaintiff's solicitor
(or see enclosed "Particulars of claim")

N2 Default summons (amount not fixed) (Order 3, rule 3(2)(a))

43

A STRAIGHTFORWARD GUIDE TO SMALL CLAIMS

Please read this page : it will help you deal with the summons

If you dispute all or part of the claim
You may be entitled to help with your legal costs. Ask about the legal aid scheme at any county court office, citizens' advice bureau, legal advice centre or firm of solicitors displaying the legal aid sign.

- Say how much you dispute in the part of the enclosed form for defending the claim and return it to the court. The court will tell you what to do next.
- If you dispute only part of the claim, you should also fill in the part of the form for admitting the claim and pay the amount admitted into court.
- If the court named on the summons is not your local county court, and/or the court for the area where the reason for the claim arose, you may write to the court named asking for the case to be transferred to the county court of your choice. You must explain your reasons for wanting the transfer. However, if the case is transferred and you later lose the case, you may have to pay more in costs.

How the claim will be dealt with if defended
If the claim is worth £1,000 or less it will be dealt with by arbitration (small claims procedure) unless the court decides the case is too difficult to be dealt with in this informal way. Costs and the grounds for setting aside an arbitration award are strictly limited. If the claim is for £1,000 or less and is not dealt with by arbitration, costs, including the costs of help from a legal representative, may be allowed.

If the claim is worth over £1000 it can still be dealt with by arbitration if either you or the plaintiff asks for it and the court approves. If your claim is dealt with by arbitration in these circumstances, costs may be allowed.

If you want to make a claim against the plaintiff
This is known as a counterclaim
Fill in the part of the enclosed form headed 'Counterclaim'. If your claim is for more than the plaintiff's claim you may have to pay a fee - the court will let you know. Unless the plaintiff admits your counterclaim there will be a hearing. The court will tell you what to do next.

If you admit the claim or any part of it
- You may pay an appropriate amount into court to compensate the plaintiff (see Payments into Court box on this page), accompanied by a notice (or letter) that the payment is in satisfaction of the claim. If the plaintiff accepts the amount paid he is also entitled to apply for his costs.
- If you need time to pay, complete the enclosed form of admission and give details of how you propose to pay the plaintiff. If your offer is accepted, the court will send an order telling you how to pay. If it is not accepted, the court will fix a rate of payment based on the details given in your form of admission and the plaintiff's comments. Judgment will be entered and you will be sent an order telling you how and when to pay.
- If the plaintiff does not accept the amount paid or offered, the court will fix a hearing to decide how much you must pay to compensate the plaintiff. The court will tell

you when the hearing, which you sho.... ....a, will take place.

General information
- If you received this summons through the post the date of service will be 7 days (for a limited company at its registered office, the second working day) after the date of posting as shown by the postmark.
- You can get help to complete the enclosed form and information about court procedures at any county court office or citizens' advice bureau. The address and telephone number of your local court is listed under 'Courts' in the phone book.
- Please address forms or letters to the Chief Clerk.
- Always quote the whole of the case number which appears at the top right corner of the front of this form; the court is unable to trace your case without it.

Registration of judgments
If the summons results in a judgment against you, your name and address may be entered in the Register of County Court Judgments. This may make it difficult for you to get credit. A leaflet giving further information can be obtained from the court.

Interest on judgments
If judgment is entered against you and is for more than £5000, the plaintiff may be entitled to interest on the total amount.

Payments into Court

You can pay the court by calling at the court office which is open 10 am to 4 pm Monday to Friday
You may only pay by:
- cash
- banker's or giro draft
- cheque supported by a cheque card
- cheque (unsupported cheques may be accepted, subject to clearance, if the Chief Clerk agrees)

Cheques and drafts must be made payable to HM Paymaster General and crossed.
Please bring this form with you.

By post
You may only pay by:
- postal order
- banker's or giro draft
- cheque (cheques may be accepted, subject to clearance, if the Chief Clerk agrees)

The payment must be made out to HM Paymaster General and crossed.
This method of payment is at your own risk.
And you must:
- pay the postage
- enclose this form
- enclose a self addressed envelope so that the court can return this form with a receipt

The court cannot accept stamps or payments by bank and giro credit transfers.

Note: You should carefully check any future forms from the court to see if payments should be made directly to the plaintiff

---

To be completed on the court copy only
Served on:
By posting on:
Officer:

This summons was returned by the Post Office marked 'Gone Away' on:

N2 Default summons (amount not fixed)

PLAINTIFF - HOW TO COMPLETE A SUMMONS FORM

Notice of Issue of Default Summons - fixed amount

To the plaintiff ('s solicitor)

In the	WOOLWICH County Court

The court office at
THE COURT HOUSE, POWIS STREET,
LONDON SE18 6JW,
is open between 10 am & 4 pm Monday to Friday
Tel: 081-854 2127

Case Number	*Always quote this*	

Plaintiff *(including ref.)*

Defendants

Your summons was issued today. The defendant has 14 days from the date of service to reply to the summons. If the date of postal service is not shown on this form you will be sent a separate notice of service (Form N222).
The defendant may either
- Pay you your total claim.
- Dispute the whole claim. The court will send you a copy of the defence and tell you what to do next.
- Admit that all the money is owed. The defendant will send you form of admission N9A. You may then ask the court to send the defendant an order to pay you the money owed by completing the request for judgment below and returning it to the court.
- Admit that only part of your claim is owed. The court will send you a copy of the reply and tell you what to do next.
- Not reply at all. You should wait 14 days from the date of service. You may then ask the court to send the defendant an order to pay you the money owed by completing the request for judgment below and returning it to the court.

Issue date	
Date of postal service	
Issue fee	£

For further information please turn over

Request for Judgment

- Tick and complete either A or B. Make sure that all the case details are given and that the judgment details at C are completed. Remember to sign and date the form. Your signature certifies that the information you have given is correct.
- If the defendant has given an address on the form of admission to which correspondence should be sent, which is different from the address shown on the summons, you will need to tell the court.

A ☐ The defendant has not replied to my summons
Complete all the judgment details at C. Decide how and when you want the defendant to pay. You can ask for the judgment to be paid by instalments or in one payment.

B ☐ The defendant admits that all the money is owed
Tick only one box below and return the completed slip to the court.

☐ I accept the defendant's proposal for payment
Complete all the judgment details at C. Say how the defendant intends to pay. The court will send the defendant an order to pay. You will also be sent a copy.

☐ The defendant has not made any proposal for payment
Complete all the judgment details at C. Say how you want the defendant to pay. You can ask for the judgment to be paid by instalments or in one payment. The court will send the defendant an order to pay. You will also be sent a copy.

☐ I do NOT accept the defendant's proposal for payment
Complete all the judgment details at C and say how you want the defendant to pay. Give your reasons for objecting to the defendant's offer of payment in the section overleaf. Return this slip to the court together with the defendant's admission N9A (or a copy). The court will fix a rate of payment and send the defendant an order to pay. You will also be sent a copy.

I certify that the information given is correct

Signed _____ Dated _____

In the	WOOLWICH County Court
Case Number	*Always quote this*
Plaintiff	
Defendant	
Plaintiff's Ref.	

C Judgment details
I would like the judgment to be paid
☐ (forthwith) *only tick this box if you intend to enforce the order right away*
☐ (by instalments of £   per month)
☐ (in full by   )

Amount of claim as stated in summons
(including interest at date of issue) _____

Interest since date of summons (if any) _____
Period _____ Rate _____ %

Court fees shown on summons _____

Solicitor's costs (if any) on issuing summons _____

Sub Total _____

Solicitor's costs (if any) on entering judgment _____

Sub Total _____

Deduct amount (if any) paid since issue _____

Amount payable by defendant _____

A STRAIGHTFORWARD GUIDE TO SMALL CLAIMS

──────────────── **Further information** ────────────────

- The summons must be served within 4 months of the date of issue (or 6 months if leave to serve out of the jurisdiction is granted under Order 8, rule 2). In exceptional circumstances you may apply for this time to be extended provided that you do so before the summons expires.

- If the defendant does not reply to the summons or if he delivers an admission without an offer of payment you may ask for judgment. If you do not ask for judgment within 12 months of the date of service the action will be struck out. It cannot be reinstated.

- You may be entitled to interest if judgment is entered against the defendant and your claim is for more than £5000.

- You should keep a record of any payments you receive from the defendant. If there is a hearing or you wish to take steps to enforce the judgment, you will need to satisfy the court about the balance outstanding. You should give the defendant a receipt and payment in cash should always be acknowledged. You should tell the defendant how much he owes if he asks.

- You **must inform the court IMMEDIATELY** if you receive any payment before a hearing date or after you have sent a request for enforcement to the court.

Objections to the defendant's proposal for payment

Case Number

PLAINTIFF - HOW TO COMPLETE A SUMMONS FORM

Notice of Arbitration Hearing

Plaintiff

Defendant

In the	Woolwich County Court
Case No.	
Plaintiff's Ref.	
Date	6 March 1995

To the plaintiff and defendant

1. Details of Hearing

This case is to be dealt with by arbitration under the small claims procedure. The notes overleaf tell you more about the hearing and what you need to do before it takes place.

The arbitration hearing will take place at The Court House, 165-167 Powis Street, Woolwich, SE18 6JW.

on , at

The time allowed for the arbitration is hours, minutes

If you do not attend, the district judge (the arbitrator) may make decisions in your absence.

If you do not wish your case to be dealt with under the informal small claims procedure, you may apply to the court. You should use form N244 which you can get free from the court office. You must say why you object to your case being dealt with as a small claims case.

The court will give you an appointment at which the district judge will consider your objections. If your case is not dealt with under the small claims procedure, costs may be allowed. That means, if you lose the case you may have to pay the other party's costs which may include the costs of help from a legal representative.

2. District Judge's Directions (What you should do)

(i) Not less than 14 days before the hearing, you must send the other party a copy of all the documents you have which you are going to use to prove your case.

(ii) Not less than 7 days before the hearing, you must send the court and the other party:
(a) a copy of any expert report you are going to use to prove your case and
(b) the name(s) and address(es) of any witness(es) you intend to use.

The court office at Woolwich County Court, The Court House, 165-167 Powis Street Woolwich SE18 6JW is open between 10 am and 4 pm Monday to Friday. When corresponding with the court, please address forms or letters to the Chief Clerk and quote the case number. Tel: 081 854 2127

Notice of arbitration hearing (small claims procedure) (Order 19, Rule 3) N18A

3. Help and Advice

- You may find it helpful to get advice about your claim and the evidence you should produce at the hearing. Many solicitors will give up to half an hour's advice for a fixed fee of £5, or you may be entitled to advice under the Legal Advice and Assistance Scheme. If expert evidence would help to prove your claim, your local Citizens Advice Bureau may be able to suggest the name of a suitable person to provide a report. They may also offer more general advice and assistance.

- You may take someone with you to the hearing to speak for you. They cannot come to the hearing alone. This person is called a 'lay representative' and can be anyone you choose, for example, your husband or wife, a relative, friend, or advice worker.

- Some lay representatives may want to be paid for helping you. You should make sure you know exactly how much this will be. Consider carefully whether your claim is worth paying that amount. Remember, you will have to pay this yourself.

- You should also remember that some lay representatives who charge for their services may not belong to any professional body. This means that if you are dissatisfied with the way they handle your case, there may be no one to whom you can complain.

- Small claims leaflet number 6 ('A defence to my claim - what happens now?') and leaflet number 7 (An arbitration hearing - how do I prepare?) will give you more information about the hearing and what you have to do.

4. Notes on the arbitration hearing

- Arbitration is an informal way of dealing with a claim. The hearing is normally held in private.

- At the hearing the district judge (the arbitrator) will decide on the best way to:
  - identify the facts and matters in dispute, and
  - make sure you have a fair and equal opportunity to present your case.

- The strict rules of evidence will not apply. The arbitrator may take into account any evidence as long as it is fair to both parties to do so.

- If you do not attend the hearing, the arbitrator will normally deal with the case in your absence. But any documents you have sent to the court will be taken into account.

- If you have a lay representative, remember to give the arbitrator form Ex83 at the beginning of the hearing. (The arbitrator can tell your lay representative to leave if he thinks he or she is behaving badly).

- If you do not have anyone to speak on your behalf, you can ask the arbitrator to help by putting questions for you.

- At the end of the hearing, the arbitrator will tell you the decision and the reasons for it.

- The decision ('award') made at the hearing is normally final. You can apply to have it set aside, but the grounds (reasons) for doing so are very limited.

5 THE DEFENDANT - HOW TO RESPOND

This chapter examines the position of a defendant. As explained above, a Summons is served by the court with forms for Admission, Defence and Counterclaim. These forms are appended to this chapter.

If you do not reply by returning the form of Admission or Defence and Counterclaim the plaintiff will be entitled to request judgment against you by returning the request he will have attached to the Plaint Note. The court will then enter "judgment–in–default" against you which means that the court will order you to either:

- pay the liquidated sum demanded, or

- in the case of an unliquidated sum, judgment will be entered against you but with damages to be assessed, with reference to the evidence given by the Plaintiff at the hearing.

If judgment in default is entered against you you must either have it set aside or pay the sum demanded. If a judgment debt is not paid a record of the fact is kept by the court on the Register of County Court Judgments for six years. This register can be referred to by people who want to know if you are creditworthy consequently you may have trouble obtaining credit or goods on hire purchase. For further details see chapter 13.

The effect of filing a Defence to a Default Summons is that a hearing will be ordered and the plaintiff loses the right to judgment in default.

THE FORM OF ADMISSION

If you admit the claim for the sum demanded, you may complete the form of Admission and post it to the Plaintiff:

- with payment, or

- with an offer for payment by instalments.

The effect of an admission is that the plaintiff will be entitled to judgment in respect of the amount you admit. The issue then is the method of payment and whether the plaintiff or the court will permit payment by instalments. It is possible just to admit part of the claim if you believe that the plaintiff is not entitled to the whole amount but in such a case, you must use the forms of defence and/or counterclaim to deny that you owe the balance of the claim. If an admission is filed but the Plaintiff does not accept your offer to pay by instalments, the court staff will set an amount with reference to the information you supply. The order to pay is issued on form N30(2), but if you object to the level of instalments, you are entitled to make an application to the district judge using form N244 for him to set a different level of instalments. The case is then transferred to your local court for a hearing.

THE FORM OF DEFENCE

If you deny that the Plaintiff's claim is valid you must file a defence. However you can only file a defence if you have a reason for disputing the plaintiff's claim and not just a reluctance to pay him. Examples are that work done was faulty, the wrong goods were supplied and that the debt is really owed to another person. You should also file a defence if you admit part of the claim and the Plaintiff will not accept your offer of part payment in full settlement. You must say why you do not owe the full amount.

PREPARING THE DEFENCE

Try and write your defence in numbered paragraphs. Look very carefully at the plaintiff's claims. Go through his paragraphs methodically and try to respond to every allegation by denying it, admitting it or saying that you do not know. If you deny something then the plaintiff must prove the allegation. If you admit something it means that the plaintiff does not have to prove that particular point and the court will take it as accepted.

It is important to also put forward your side of the story summarising what really happened and why it means you are not liable to the Plaintiff as they claim. However, remember that if you are making a claim of your own against the plaintiff, for example for damages, then the allegations that relate to this should be made in the counter claim and not in the defence.

As well as putting forward an alternative version or interpretation of events you can also take issue with the amount of damage the plaintiff claims to have suffered. For example you might say that goods which were damaged are not as valuable as the plaintiff claims or his injury was not as serious as the plaintiff suggests. You are also entitled to expect a plaintiff to mitigate these losses. This means that they should take all reasonable steps to minimise the loss caused even if there has been fault on the part of the defendant, for example by breach of contract. They cannot recover loss which the defendant can prove resulted from a failure to mitigate. You can dispute the amount of loss suffered while still denying that you were in any way responsible for any loss at all. This is a prudent course of action as it may mean that if you are unsuccessful in your defence you do not have to pay the full amount the plaintiff is seeking.

For examples of defence see Appendix 1.

THE FORM OF COUNTERCLAIM

If you wish to make a claim against the Plaintiff, you may file a counterclaim. This is equivalent to issuing your own summons against the plaintiff. Thus, while the defence answers the plaintiff's claim the counterclaim is a separate action, that will be considered with the original claim. As with a plaintiff's original claim you request either a fixed amount as damages to be assessed. If the counterclaim is in excess of the small claims limit this does not prevent the case being automatically referred to arbitration but it is one of the factors a district judge can take into account when considering whether the case should proceed as a small claim. A court fee will be payable if the counterclaim exceeds the claim against you, see Appendix 2.

A counterclaim should be made in the same way as the Particulars contained in the Summons (see Chapter 4). Write in numbered paragraphs which state clearly what you claim, why the plaintiff is liable and what compensation you require. The plaintiff is entitled to file a Defence and Reply to a counterclaim. It is advisable to do so especially if the counterclaim raises any new issues. However the allegations in a counterclaim are treated as denied even if a Defence and Reply is not filed.

SETTING ASIDE A DEFAULT JUDGMENT

If a Default Judgment is made against you when you have a defence, you may apply to the Court for the judgment to be "set aside" by using form N244, but you must establish grounds for the application, for example, that you have a defence or that you did not receive the summons in the post. The court will arrange an arbitration hearing. You must give reasons for your failure to file a defence and convince the judge that your defence is genuine.

THIRD PARTY PROCEEDINGS

A defendant who holds a third party entirely or partly responsible for the plaintiff's loss is entitled to join the third party in the action by issuing a Third Party Notice. Leave of the court is required to issue the Notice if the defence has been filed.

An example of where you might want to join a third party is if the plaintiff brings an action seeking compensation for damage to his car caused by you driving into the back of it. But you only hit the plaintiff's vehicle because your car was shunted forward as a result of being hit by a third party's car. In such circumstances you would want the third party to be joined in the action as he is the person who is really responsible for the damage.

Now please read the **KEY POINTS** from chapter 5 overleaf.

KEY POINTS

- If you receive a Summons, you must take the appropriate action or judgment will be issued against you.

- If judgment is entered, you can apply for it to be set aside. This means that you have permission to enter a defence.

- If you think that you have a claim against the plaintiff, you must complete the form of counterclaim to make your claim. Do not make the claim in your Form of Defence.

- If you admit the claim but believe that another person is responsible, you can issue Third Party Proceedings.

Forms Appended

I. Form of Admission Defence and Counterclaim (Form N9A)

II. Form of Defence and Counterclaim (Form N9B)

5 DEFENDANT - HOW TO RESPOND

Admission

When to fill in this form
- Only fill in this form if you are admitting all or some of the claim and you are asking for time to pay
- If you are disputing the claim or you wish to pay the amount claimed, read the back of the summons

How to fill in this form
- Tick the correct boxes and give as much information as you can. Then sign and date the form.
- Make your offer of payment in box 11 on the back of this form. If you make no offer the plaintiff will decide how you should pay.
- You can get help to complete this form at any county court office or citizens' advice bureau.

Where to send this form
- If you admit the claim in full
  Send the completed form to the address shown at box (2) on the front of the summons. If there is no address in box (2) send the form to the address in box (1).
- If you admit only part of the claim
  Send the form to the court at the address given on the summons, together with the white defence form (N9B).

What happens next
- If you admit the claim in full and offer to pay
  If the plaintiff accepts your offer, judgement will be entered and you will be sent an order telling you how and when to pay. If the plaintiff does not accept your offer, the court will fix a rate of payment based on the details you have given in this form and the plaintiff's comments. Judgement will be entered and you will be sent an order telling you how and when to pay.
- If you admit only part of the claim
  The court will tell you what to do next.

How much of the claim do you admit?
- [ ] I admit the full amount claimed as shown on the summons **or**
- [ ] I admit the amount of $ [   ]

1 Personal details

Surname [   ]
Forename [   ]
[ ] Mr   [ ] Mrs   [ ] Miss   [ ] Ms
[ ] Married   [ ] Single   [ ] Other (specify) [   ]
Age [   ]
Address
[   ]
Postcode [   ]

In the WOOLWICH **County Court**

Case Number [Always quote this] [   ]
Plaintiff *(including ref.)* [   ]
Defendant [   ]

2 Dependants *(people you look after financially)*
Number of children in each age group
under 11 [ ]   11-15 [ ]   16-17 [ ]   18 & over [ ]
Other dependants *(give details)* [   ]

3 Employment
- [ ] I am employed as a [   ]
  My employer is [   ]
  Jobs other than main job *(give details)* [   ]
- [ ] I am self employed as a [   ]
  Annual turnover is..................... $ [   ]
  - [ ] I am not in arrears with my national insurance contributions, income tax and VAT
  - [ ] I am in arrears and I owe.......... $ [   ]
  Give details of:
  (a) contracts and other work in hand
  (b) any sums due for work done [   ]
- [ ] I have been unemployed for [years] [months]
- [ ] I am a pensioner

4 Bank account and savings
- [ ] I have a bank account
  - [ ] The account is in credit by..... $ [   ]
  - [ ] The account is overdrawn by.... $ [   ]
- [ ] I have a savings or building society account
  The amount in the account is .... $ [   ]

5 Property
I live in   [ ] my own property   [ ] lodgings
            [ ] jointly owned property [ ] council property
            [ ] rented property

N9A Form of admission and statement of means to accompany Form N1 (Order 9, rule 2)

A STRAIGHTFORWARD GUIDE TO SMALL CLAIMS

6 Income

My usual take home pay *(including overtime, commission, bonuses etc)* £____ per ____
Income support £____ per ____
Child benefit(s) £____ per ____
Other state benefit(s) £____ per ____
My pension(s) £____ per ____
Others living in my home give me £____ per ____
Other income *(please specify below)*
£____ per ____
£____ per ____
£____ per ____

Total income £____ per ____

7 Expenses

(Do not include any expenses paid by other members of the household out of their own income)

I have regular expenses as follows:

Mortgage *(including second mortgage)* £____ per ____
Rent £____ per ____
Community charge £____ per ____
Gas £____ per ____
Electricity £____ per ____
Water charges £____ per ____

TV rental and licence £____ per ____
HP repayments £____ per ____
Mail order £____ per ____

Housekeeping, food, school meals £____ per ____
Travelling expenses £____ per ____
Children's clothing £____ per ____
Maintenance payments £____ per ____
Others *(not court orders or credit debts listed in boxes 9 and 10)*
£____ per ____
£____ per ____
£____ per ____

Total expenses £____ per ____

8 Priority debts *(This section is for arrears only. Do not include regular payments here (see box 7))*

Rent arrears £____ per ____
Mortgage arrears £____ per ____
Community charge arrears £____ per ____
Water charges arrears £____ per ____
Fuel debts: Gas £____ per ____
Electricity £____ per ____
Other £____ per ____
Maintenance arrears £____ per ____
Others *(please specify below)*
£____ per ____
£____ per ____

Total priority debts £____ per ____

9 Court orders

Court	Case No.	£	per

Total court order instalments £____ per ____

Of the payments above, I am behind with payments to *(please list)*

10 Credit debts

Loans and credit card debts *(please list)*

£____ per ____
£____ per ____
£____ per ____

Of the payments above, I am behind with payments to *(please list)*

11 Do you wish to make an offer of payment?

• *If you take away the totals of boxes 7, 8 and 9 and the payments you are making in box 10 from the total in box 6 you will get some idea of the sort of sum you should offer. The offer you make should be one you can afford.*

☐ I can pay the amount admitted on _____
or
☐ I can pay by monthly instalments of £____

12 Declaration

I declare that the details I have given above are true to the best of my knowledge

Signed _____ Dated _____

Position *(firm or company)* _____

5 DEFENDANT - HOW TO RESPOND

Defence and Counterclaim

When to fill in this form
- Only fill in this form if you wish to dispute all or part of the claim and/or make a claim against the plaintiff (counterclaim).

How to fill in this form
- Please check that the correct case details are shown on this form. You must ensure that all the boxes at the top right of this form are completed. You can obtain the correct names and numbers from the summons. The court cannot trace your case without this information.
- Follow the instructions given in each section. Tick the correct boxes and give the other details asked for.
- If you wish only to make a claim against the plaintiff (counterclaim) go to section 5.
- Complete and sign section 6 before returning this form.

Where to send this form
- Send or take this form immediately to the court office at the address shown above.
- If you admit part of the claim and you are asking for time to pay, you will also need to fill in the blue admission form (N9A) and send both reply forms to the court.
- Keep the summons and a copy of this defence; you may need them.

Legal Aid
- You may be entitled to legal aid. Ask about the legal aid scheme at any county court office, citizen's advice bureau, legal advice centre or firm of solicitors displaying this legal aid sign.

What happens next
- If you complete box 3 on this form, the court will ask the plaintiff to confirm that he has received payment. If he tells the court that you have not paid, the court will tell you what you should do.
- If you complete box 4 or 5, the court will tell you what you should do.
- If the summons is not from your local county court, it will automatically be transferred to your local court.

1 How much of the claim do you dispute?

☐ I dispute the full amount claimed *(go to section 2)*
or
☐ I admit the amount of £ _____ and I dispute the balance

If you dispute only part of the claim you must either:
- pay the amount admitted to the person named at the address for payment in box (2) on the front of the summons or if there is no address in box (2), send the money to the address in box (1) (see How to Pay on the back of the summons). Then send this defence to the court.
or
- complete the blue admission form and send it to the court with this defence.

Tick whichever applies

☐ I paid the amount admitted on _____
or
☐ I enclose the completed form of admission
(go to section 2)

In the WOOLWICH **County Court**

Case Number *Always quote this*

Plaintiff *(including ref.)*

Defendant

The court office is open from 10am to 4pm Monday to Friday
COURT HOUSE
165 POWIS STREET
WOOLWICH
LONDON
SE18 6JW

2 Arbitration under the small claims procedure
How the claim will be dealt with if defended

If the claim is for £1,000 or less it will be dealt with by arbitration (small claims procedure) unless the court decides the case is too difficult to be dealt with in this informal way. Costs and the grounds for setting aside an arbitration award are strictly limited. If the claim is for £1,000 or less and is not dealt with by arbitration, costs, including the costs of a legal representative, may be allowed.

If the claim is for over £1,000 it can still be dealt with by arbitration if either you or the plaintiff asks for it and the court approves. If the claim is dealt with by arbitration in these circumstances, costs may be allowed.

Please tick this box if the claim is worth over £1,000 and you would like it dealt with by arbitration. ☐
(go on to section 3)

3 Do you dispute this claim because you have already paid it? *Tick whichever applies*

☐ No *(go to section 4)*

☐ Yes I paid £ _____ to the plaintiff
on _____ *(before the summons was issued)*

Give details of where and how you paid it in the box below *(then go to section 6)*

A STRAIGHTFORWARD GUIDE TO SMALL CLAIMS

Case No.

4 If you dispute the claim for reasons other than payment, what are your reasons?
Use the box below to give full details. *(If you need to continue on a separate sheet, put the case number in the top right hand corner.)*

5 If you wish to make a claim against the plaintiff (counterclaim)

If your claim is for a specific sum of money, how much are you claiming? £

- If your claim against the plaintiff is for more than the plaintiff's claim against you, you may have to pay a fee. Ask at your local court office whether a fee is payable.

- You may not be able to make a counterclaim where the plaintiff is the Crown (e.g. a Government Department). Ask at your local county court office for further information.

What are your reasons for making the counterclaim?

- Use the box opposite to give full details. *(If you need to continue on a separate sheet, put the case number in the top right hand corner.)*

(go on to section 6)

6 Signed
(To be signed by you or by your solicitor)

Position
(firm or company)

Give an address to which notices about this case can be sent to you

Dated

Postcode

6 EVIDENCE

Our legal system is in general adversarial and not inquisitorial. This means that both parties to a dispute must present a case to a judge who, although he is an experienced lawyer, acts as an impartial observer. The small claims procedure is an exception to this rule in that the judge will be more involved. He will ask questions and try and find out what he needs to know. Nevertheless it is the responsibility of the parties to supply the evidence for the judge to consider.

TYPES OF EVIDENCE

Evidence is information which can be presented to the court to enable the judge to decide on the probability of a claim which has been made being correct or true. Evidence can take a number of different forms:

- Oral Evidence. Both the plaintiff and the defendant will be able to give evidence by speaking to the District Judge, giving their account of events and presenting their arguments. They can also call witnesses to attend court and give oral evidence about any relevant fact of which they have knowledge. If a witness is unwilling to attend the hearing, you are entitled to compel their attendance by issuing a witness summons (Form N20). This must be done at least seven days before the hearing and it will mean that you have to pay the witnesses expenses and the cost of their travel to and from the court. Court staff will tell you how much this is. If you are successful and win the case you should be able to recover the cost of the witnesses travelling and overnight expenses reasonably incurred and £50 for their loss of earnings from your opponent.

- Witness Statements. Witnesses who can not come to the hearing can give their evidence in writing. They should give their full name and address and sign and date their statement. Such evidence can be very useful but, depending on the circumstances, it is likely to carry less weight than direct oral testimony because the other party and the judge do not have the opportunity to question the witness, and because seeing someone give their evidence would help the district judge to decide how credible he finds that witness. On the other hand, if you get your witness to make a statement prior to the hearing and ask your opponent if they will accept that the evidence contained in the statement is correct you may be able to save the cost and trouble of bringing the witness to court. Witness statements are also useful where you have a number of witnesses who are going to say the same thing. You can ask one of them to attend the hearing and request that the others make statements. Photocopies of witness statements should be given to the other party prior to the hearing in accordance with the court's directions.

- Documentary Evidence. This includes things like contracts, letters, a returned cheque, estimates, delivery notes, receipts, diary entries, guarantees and photographs. Judges are usually faced with parties giving contradictory oral evidence and the difficult job of choosing between them, so documentary evidence which supports one account rather than the other is very helpful. It is often a good idea to take photographs in preparation for the case. For example if you are making a claim against a builder who you say has done bad work or you have been physically injured then having a photograph of things like the bad work, the injury and the scene of the accident will not only improve your credibility but may also help the judge to form a clearer picture of what went on and what is at issue. You can also use or draw up plans or maps to help you explain what happened. This is particularly useful in disputes about road accidents. It may save time if you can get your opponent to agree in writing before the hearing that your plans are accurate.

- Other Physical Evidence and Site Visits. In addition to documents you can use other physical evidence to support your claims. For example if the dispute is about reasonably small and portable goods you could take the goods in question, or a sample, along to the arbitration to show that they are faulty in some way. In some circumstances the arbitrator may want to visit the scene of the accident or the place where unsatisfactory work was done, or to go and see an object which cannot be brought to the court. This is known as a site visit and both the plaintiff and the defendant will be given notice in advance and the opportunity to attend.

- Expert Evidence. This is required when it is necessary to decide a question which needs specialist or technical knowledge which the arbitrator is unlikely to have. For example a surveyor may give an opinion on building works and a doctor will be a suitable expert in personal injury cases. When a matter calls for expert evidence only a suitably qualified person can give it. This does not necessarily mean that they must have formal qualifications although these are usually expected and it may be difficult to satisfy a judge that a witness is an expert if he does not have formal qualifications.

- To find an expert you can contact the relevant professional or trade association and ask for a recommendation or a Citizens Advice Bureau or Trading Standards Officer may be able to help you find a suitable person. It is important not to use an expert you already have close connections with such as a relative or friend because the arbitrator is likely to give less weight to the evidence of an expert who is not entirely independent.

- When you have found a suitable expert ask him to write a report. Explain clearly what you want and what is at issue This will ensure he answers the important questions and also that he does not do unnecessary work which will increase your costs. It may be possible for both you and your opponent to minimise your expenses by agreeing to use the same expert. In which case you should agree in advance what questions you want the expert to answer and what evidence he will see. Another alternative is for you to ask the court to appoint an expert to act as the arbitrator in place of the District Judge. In such circumstances you and your opponent would share the costs.If you already have a pre-arbitration appointment you can request that the District Judge agree to this procedure at that hearing. Alternatively you can apply on Form N244 and you will be given an appointment.

* Remember to give copies of expert reports to your opponent and to the court before the arbitration date in accordance with the courts directions.

THE BURDEN OF PROOF

It is the Plaintiff who brings the case to court and who makes allegations about the defendant or his conduct and it is for the plaintiff to establish that these claims are true. In legal terms it is said that he bears the burden of proof.

Although the plaintiff formally bears the burden of proof, on a practical level both the plaintiff and the defendant can be subject to the "onus of proof". This means that when the plaintiff has made a plausible allegation and substantiated his claims, for example producing evidence that goods were delivered but not paid for then the onus is on the defendant to give an answer or give an explanation. The defendant might produce evidence of payment. This would then put the onus of proof back on the Plaintiff. The Plaintiff could allege that the payments were for other invoices and so on.

Because the plaintiff bears the burden of proof, if at the end of the hearing the arbitrator finds that the plaintiff's and the defendant's arguments are of equal strength he must decide in favour of the defendant and dismiss the summons. When he is making a counterclaim the defendant bears the burden of proof in respect of this part of the case.

THE STANDARD OF PROOF

It is unlikely that either party will be able to prove their case with 100% certainty but this is not required. In order to discharge the burden of proof the plaintiff (or in a counterclaim the defendant) must show he is right "on the balance of probabilities".This means that the arbitrator must be satisfied that what he is claiming is more likely than not to be correct. The criminal standard of proof, that a case must be proved "beyond reasonable doubt" does not normally have any application in small claims.

WHAT YOU MUST PROVE

At the hearing the plaintiff must prove each of the statements made in his particulars of claim. He must also prove the level of loss he has suffered because if he is successful the court will award damages to compensate him for his loss, not to punish the defendant. The plaintiff does not have to prove any of the particulars which are admitted by the defendant in his defence. It is also the plaintiff's responsibility to prove that the defendant received the summons. This is relevant when the defendant does not attend the hearing or attends but denies service, but it is not relevant when the defendant has returned one of the forms of admission, defence and counterclaim.

The Defendant must prove all of the allegations he makes in the counterclaim and the level of loss he suffered. He should also bring any evidence available to him which disproves or undermines any of the plaintiff's claims in the particulars of claim, including those about the extent of the loss he has suffered, or which supports the defendant's alternative account of events.

THE RULES OF EVIDENCE

The rules of evidence which normally govern what evidence is admissible, which means what the judge will consider and take into account, do not apply to small claims.

Now read the **KEY POINTS** from chapter 6.

KEY POINTS

- At the hearing, the Plaintiff must present a case. The judge is not there to do this for you. His role is to arbitrate and decide who has the strongest case.

- "Small claims" arbitrations do not follow the strict rules of evidence and court procedure, although the basic undercurrent of these rules apply. This is because complicated legal issues rarely have a role to play in a claim below £1,000. The main issues are usually the facts and, in general, a determined plaintiff can work out what facts are relevant and how to prove them. Due to the informal nature of "small claims" and to encourage legal representation to be dispensed with, the judge will be prepared to adopt a less passive role in a "small claims" arbitration.

- The ease with which you can prove a case depends to a great extent on the documentary evidence you have. It is therefore important to have an administrative system which guarantees clear correspondence, signed contracts, and signed delivery notes.

- The judge will decide on the basis of the oral evidence and documents presented to him, and the law.

- Legal costs are not awarded but certain costs may be awarded in favour of the successful party.

7 THE COSTS OF ARBITRATION

COUNTY COURT FEES

These are fees which must be paid to the court to commence and enforce your claim. When you issue a summons and you are only claiming money the amount of the fee is determined by the size of your claim, as outlined below:

	Claim	Fee
up to	£ 100	£10
	£ 200	£20
	£ 300	£30
	£ 400	£40
	£ 500	£50
	£ 600	£60
	£1,000	£65
	£3,000	£70

To issue proceedings where you are claiming something other than money, such as an injunction, the fee is £65. You can include a claim for money without paying an additional fee.

COUNTERCLAIMS

If you are making a counterclaim you will have to pay a fee if the amount you are claiming is more than the sum being claimed from you. To calculate the amount you should work out the ordinary fee for a claim of that size and then deduct the fee which the plaintiff has already paid. You will have to pay the
difference. For example if the counterclaim is £500 the ordinary fee for a claim of that size would be £50. However if the plaintiff's claim is for £400 that will have been subject to a fee of £40. The difference of £10 is what the defendant must pay. The same method of calculation is used to work out the fees payable for the enforcement of counterclaims.

Service by a Court Bailiff

Having documents served by a court bailiff carries a fee of £10 for each person served. This applies even if a number of people are served at the same address.

Setting Aside Awards

If you make an application to set aside an award made by an arbitrator a fee of £20 will be payable.

Enforcing Judgments

If you have succeeded in obtaining a judgment against someone and they have not complied with the courts order you may issue enforcement proceedings to make them fulfil their obligations. The fees are:

A warrant to recover a sum not more than £125	£20
A warrant to recover a sum over £125	£40
A warrant for the recovery of property (a possession)	£80
To issue an application for an attachment of earnings order	£50
To issue an application for a charging order	£50
To issue an application for a garnishee order	£25
To issue a judgment summons	£25
To issue an application for an oral examination	£30

You do not have to pay court fees if you are receiving income support at the time the fee is paid. This exemption applies even if you are receiving legal advice and assistance under the "Green form Scheme" but not if you are in receipt of legal representation under Part IV of the Legal Aid Act 1988 for the purpose of proceedings. You may also be exempt from paying fees, at the discretion of the Chief Clerk, if you can show that paying the fee would cause undue hardship because of the exceptional circumstances of the case.

Recovering Costs From Your Opponent

Small claims are an exception to the usual practice where in general if you win your case your opponent pays you costs. In small claims even if you are entirely successful only a few of your possible expenses will be recoverable. They are:

- the costs which were stated on the summons or which would have been on the summons if the claim had been for a liquidated sum;

- up to £200 in respect of the fees of an expert. Inclusive of VAT;

- up to £260 for legal advice obtained to bring or defend a claim for an injunction, specific performance or similar relief. Inclusive of VAT;

- up to £50 in respect of a party's or a witness's loss of earnings when attending a hearing;

- any expenses which have been reasonably incurred by a party or a witness in travelling to and from the hearing or in staying away from home;

- the costs of enforcing the award;

- such further costs as a district judge may direct where there has been unreasonable conduct on the part of the opposite party in relation to the proceedings or a claim that was made. An example of unreasonable conduct would be the fabrication of a wholly untruthful defence.

LEGAL AID

The Legal Aid green form scheme is available to pay for a limited amount of advice and assistance from a solicitor for those with sufficiently low incomes. It does not cover representation at the hearing or court fees but might provide payment for expert evidence. Consult a solicitor for advice about whether or not you are eligible under the green form scheme.

The Legal Aid Board's guidance on the availability of ordinary legal aid (non-green form scheme), which could include representation at the hearing, suggests that it should not be granted within the small claims procedure "unless there are exceptional circumstances and there will be a tangible benefit to an assisted person". If you think you might be eligible consult a solicitor for advice. You should bear in mind that if you do receive legal aid there will be a statutory charge. This means that the costs you incur will be paid out of any damages or compensation you receive and you will only be able to keep what is left over.

7 THE COSTS OF ARBITRATION

INJUNCTIONS AND SPECIFIC PERFORMANCE

The provision of the county court rule which governs automatic reference to arbitration refers to actions where there is a "sum claimed" or "amount involved", thus it is arguable that if you are not claiming money but only seeking an injunction or specific performance your case should not be automatically referred to arbitration. If the case is not dealt with as a small claim this could mean it would be easier for you to claim legal aid, and more importantly that if you win your case you could recover your costs from your opponent. Consequently if you are claiming a small amount in damages with your injunction it may actually save you money to forego the damages claim. Such considerations can be complex and difficult and you would put yourself at risk of paying your opponents costs if you lose so take advice from a solicitor on this question. Remember £260 spent on advance is recoverable even if the case proceeds as a small claim.

Housing Matters

If you have a housing dispute for example, for nuisance or disrepair, you may be able to bring a claim in the magistrates court under the Environmental Protection Act 1990 as an alternative to arbitration. You can claim up to £5,000 in damages and get a nuisance order which is equivalent to specific performance. Legal aid is not available but if you are successful you can claim your legal costs from your opponent.

Avoiding Arbitration

If your case is a strong one and you would like it to be heard in a county court rather than as a small claim so that you will be able to recover your costs if you win refer to the section "is it a small claim?"

in chapter 1 and consider whether any of the justifications for a trial apply to your case. However beware of inflating your claim.

Now read the **KEY POINTS** from chapter 7.

7 THE COSTS OF ARBITRATION

KEY POINTS

- A fee must be paid to commence your claim.

- If you are making a counter claim you will have to pay a fee if the amount you are claiming is more than the sum being paid from you.

- Generally, in Small Claims actions you cannot recover your costs.

- Legal Aid may be available in certain circumstances, but not for court representation.

8 PREPARING FOR THE ARBITRATION HEARING

PRELIMINARY APPOINTMENTS

The court controls what steps should be taken before the hearing by issuing "directions". The usual directions for an arbitration are listed in chapter 7, but sometimes these standard directions are not adequate. Either party can make an application to the court on form N244 for a preliminary appointment at which the party may request additional directions. This is not usually necessary in small claims proceedings but may be useful in complex cases such as personal injury claims. The other party may oppose your application or not attend the hearing. If at all possible try and agree the directions with your opponent then both parties can write to the court asking for the same direction. In nearly all cases, the court will grant any directions which both parties request.

A preliminary appointment can also be used to claim that the summons does not establish a claim as the defence does not present a proper defence. It would also be an opportunity to argue that claim does not really fall within the small claims limit or that it should be transferred to the county court for one of the other reasons outlined in chapter 1.

A preliminary appointment is informal and takes place in a private room with a district judge and the litigants present. Remember, a preliminary appointment is not the arbitration. Beyond establishing whether or not you have an arguable claim or defence the judge will not consider the merits of the case at this stage so you do not need to take along witnesses or to be fully prepared to argue your case at this stage.

Failure to Attend a Preliminary Appointment

If the plaintiff fails to attend, the judge will probably strike the case out. If the defendant does not attend, the judge could either issue direction or strike out the defence, or if the admission is filed, allow the plaintiff to prove the level of loss suffered.

Trial Date and Time Estimates

If it has not done so already the court will set a date for the arbitration. If you cannot attend on the date set inform the court immediately. The judge who issues the directions will give a time estimate of how long he expects the case to last. If the time estimate is too short, write to the court and/or telephone the listings clerk because otherwise the judge may not have time to hear your case in full and you will have to go back on another date. Another appointment is unlikely to be immediately available so this will mean you have to wait longer to get the case resolved. Either the plaintiff or the defendant can ask for more time. Allow plenty of time for your witnesses to give their evidence and to be questioned by your opponent.

Complying with Directions

It is essential that you comply with the arbitrator's directions concerning what should be done and exchanged before the trial. Failure to exchange documentary evidence and expert reports may

8 *PREPARING FOR THE ARBITRATION HEARING*

mean that you cannot use such evidence during the arbitration hearing and this could seriously harm your prospects
of success.

YOUR OWN PREPARATIONS FOR THE ARBITRATION

Although small claims hearings are fairly informal many people find the prospect of presenting their case to the arbitrator makes them feel rather anxious. The better you prepare before the hearing the more confident you will be when you attend the arbitration.

- The Plaintiff. You will have to be prepared to introduce the case to the arbitrator by telling him what it is about, what happened, why the defendant was at fault and what is at issue or in dispute. It is a good idea to write a list of important points in the order you want to mention them so that you do not forget things or repeat yourself. Look back at your particulars of claim and the defence to make sure you have not overlooked anything. If you can, find an obliging friend, practice explaining your case and ask them if what you say is clear and easy to follow.

- The Defendant. You will have to respond to the plaintiff's claim however you will know in advance what this is and so will be able to predict much of what the plaintiff will say. Look at the particulars of claim and the documents you receive from the plaintiff such as expert's reports. Make your own note of the key allegations being made against you and then be prepared to outline your defence to the arbitrator rebutting each of these allegations. Make a list of the points you intend to make in order. You may benefit from practice in explaining your defence to a friend or relative.

- Preparing to deal with witnesses. Once you have outlined your claim or defence you will have the opportunity to call witnesses to give evidence. Before the arbitration reflect on why you are calling each witness and what you hope they will say that will strengthen your case or weaken your opponents. Prepare a few questions with which you could prompt them to discuss the relevant matter without actually giving the court the evidence yourself. For example: "What did you see after the red car came around the corner of Smith Street?" is preferable to "The Defendant drove around the corner of Smith Street too fast, swerved all over the road and then negligently drove over my bicycle, didn't he?" The arbitrator will have already heard your account of events, he now wants to hear from the witness. You may undermine the strength of his evidence if you, in effect, tell him what to say. Preparing questions in advance will help you to resist the natural temptation to try and give the witness's evidence for him.

- You will also get an opportunity to question your opponent's witnesses, this is known as cross–examination. When doing this the recommendation about not giving evidence for them does not apply, in that you can make a statement of fact such as "the defendant was going too fast wasn't he?" or "the plaintiff had left his bicycle in the middle of the road hadn't he?" and ask them for a yes or no answer. Try to think in advance of anything which weakens or discredits their evidence. For example that they could not have had a very good view of the accident, they are in business with your opponent, or their memory of events is imperfect on one point so should not be relied on in relation to another question.

- In general when you are preparing for the hearing it is a good idea to try and step back from the case. This is difficult as you will naturally feel strongly about your claim or defence but if you can try and see it from an impartial viewpoint and then try and think from your opponent's perspective you may get a clearer appreciation of the strengths and weaknesses of your case and be better able to predict what will be raised at the arbitration.

8 PREPARING FOR THE ARBITRATION HEARING

- In preparation for the hearing have plenty of copies of the documents with you because you may have to supply them to the arbitrator or your opponent and photocopying at court costs £1 for every sheet.

It could also be worth your while trying to reach agreement with your opponent before the arbitration hearing.

Now read the **KEY POINTS** from chapter 8.

KEY POINTS

- A preliminary appointment can be used to request further directions or to ask that the case be transferred to the county court.

- Failure to exchange documentary evidence and expert reports may mean that you cannot use such evidence during the arbitration hearing.

- If you cannot attend on the appointed day or if the time estimate is too short, write to the chief clerk and telephone the listing clerk.

- The better you prepare before the hearing the more confident you will be when you attend the arbitration.

9 SETTLING THE DISPUTE

It may be worth your while to try and reach a compromise with your opponent and to settle the case without an arbitration hearing. This is because all litigation contains some element of risk. However much you believe in your own case there is almost always a chance that the arbitrator's decision could go against you. By reaching a settlement you save yourself the risk of losing completely in return for conceding something to your opponent. You also save yourself the time and trouble involved in arguing the merits of the case in front of the arbitrator. Think carefully about the strengths and weaknesses of your case, then decide what you would be prepared to accept. It is important to be realistic.

HOW TO NEGOTIATE A SETTLEMENT

If you want to reach a settlement you can write to your opponent and make them an offer. Letters concerning settlements are usually headed "without prejudice". This means "without prejudice to the position of the writer if the terms he proposes are not accepted". The practical effect heading your letter "without prejudice" is that if your opponent refuses your offer or ignores it then the letter and its contents cannot be used as evidence. If the offer is accepted by your opponent it becomes a binding agreement to settle the action and it can be revealed to the arbitrator. If you do not want to be bound by an offer you could put it as a question first. For example, "If I were to offer you £1,000 what would your reaction be?" and say that you are not making an offer which you intend to be bound by without further agreement. The words "without prejudice" should only be used on letters intended to assist in settling the dispute and cannot be used to make other documents inadmissible as evidence.

You could also write to your opponent and ask if they would be prepared to discuss the case on the telephone or arrange a meeting in the hope that you can negotiate a settlement. If you do not know your opponent well exercise caution and common sense and only meet them somewhere you will be safe.

When entering into negotiations it is important to be prepared. It is a good idea to write down three figures in advance. Firstly, an opening offer or request which might be slightly more than you expect to receive or less than you expect to pay, secondly the figure you would be happy to accept or to pay and thirdly your bottom line which is the minimum you would accept or the maximum you would pay your opponent. It is particularly important to decide on the final figure and keep it in mind so that you cannot be pushed into an unfavourable settlement by an aggressive opponent. There is no point in reaching a settlement for its own sake. Only settle the dispute if you feel you have something to gain by doing so.

When to Negotiate

You are free to negotiate at any time, from before the start of legal proceedings until the arbitrator makes his judgment. In small claims the disclosure of evidence normally takes place only one or two weeks before the date set for arbitration. If you feel that seeing your opponent's documents and expert's reports is likely to effect your view of the strength or weakness of their case it may be worth waiting until you have received copies before reaching any agreement.

9 SETTLING THE DISPUTE

When to Accept an Offer

If your opponent makes you an offer of settlement consider what his motives may be. If it is very low it could be that he has misjudged the strength of his own case but alternatively he may have spotted a genuine weakness in your case which you have not noticed. You are free to ask him why he thinks that amount is reasonable. If the offer is high you will naturally want to come to a decision quickly in case it is withdrawn but you should not necessarily accept it immediately. There may be a weakness in his case you do not yet know about or yours might be stronger than you think. If a relatively large sum is involved it might be worth taking advice on whether or not to accept it.

Consent Orders

The Court will normally approve a settlement which both sides accept. This is achieved by a Consent Order. A formal form of consent may be signed and filed with the Court any time before the hearing. In a small claim arbitration, it would be sufficient for both sides to write to the court outlining their agreement or for one party to set out the agreed compromise and the other to sign at the foot of the letter. A consent order must be approved by the judge.

At the hearing, if a compromise is agreed, the judge would record the agreement so that a consent order or judgment is drawn up by the court.

Withdrawing the Summons

If a settlement has been agreed, the plaintiff may file a Notice of Discontinuance (Form N297) and a certificate saying that the defendant has been informed of withdrawal of the Summons. The case would be ended without a court order. This option may be suitable if the Plaintiff simply abandons the case altogether, or if the defendant pays an agreed sum in one payment. If instalments are agreed, the Plaintiff is better off with a court order which is capable of enforcement. A consent order would be preferable to a discontinuance.

Now read the **KEY POINTS** from chapter 9.

9 SETTLING THE DISPUTE

KEY POINTS

- You should try to reach a compromise with your opponent and to settle the case without an arbitration hearing.

- You are free to negotiate at any time, from before the start of legal proceedings until the arbitrator makes his judgment.

- Consider an offer carefully before accepting it.

- If a settlement has been reached, the Plaintiff may file a notice of discontinuance - withdrawing the case.

10 REPRESENTATION

The small claims procedure is designed with the intention that people will be able to conduct their own case and legal representation should not usually be necessary. Consequently you are allowed to have a lay representative to state your case for you, perhaps a friend or relative who feels more confident about speaking to the judge. A lay representative cannot be heard if the person he represents does not attend the hearing and the arbitrator has the right to exclude him for misconduct. If the party to the case is a company it will need the arbitrator's permission for it to be represented by anyone other than a lawyer, for example a director. Acting as a lay representative does not prevent someone from also giving evidence as a witness. An example of this would be where one spouse represents the other and both of them have witnessed the events in issue. In such circumstances the arbitrator should warn them that this may affect the weight which the court gives to the lay representative's evidence. There is no right to a lay representative where the claim has been referred to arbitration voluntarily. If you would like to have a lay representative fill in form Ex 83 to let the court know.

Parties to a small claim are also entitled to employ a solicitor if they wish. However they will be unable to recover the cost of legal representation from their opponent if they are successful and so they will have to pay the costs themselves. Legal aid is not normally available for representation in small claims. If a party is unable to properly represent themselves in a small claim, for example as a result of a physical disability, poor sight, pronounced stammer or inability to read, these circumstances can be taken into account by the district judge when deciding whether or not the case should be automatically referred to arbitration or whether it should go to a county court trial for which legal aid may be available. If you feel you are unable to represent yourself inform the court well before the arbitration date and ask for a preliminary appointment for directions. You could also apply for legal aid on the grounds that your circumstances are exceptional.

It is not possible to have the case sent to the county court on the grounds that one party is represented and the other is not. Inequality of representation can be worrying and intimidating for people bringing their own small claim, but if you are in this situation do not panic. It is unlikely to make a great deal of difference as the arbitrator will take a fairly active role to ensure that you are not unfairly disadvantaged by a lack of legal expertise. Arbitrators are all experienced lawyers who will be well able to assess the validity of claims your opponent may make about the law.

11 ARBITRATION AND JUDGMENT

You will receive notification of the date, time and place set for the arbitration hearing from the court when the defence has been filed. If you have not been there before allow plenty of time to find the court. What you think of as your local court may well be a magistrates court or a Crown court. Your arbitration will be heard in the county court. You may wear what you wish but it is a good idea to dress smartly to make a favourable impression on the arbitrator. Bring the originals and spare copies of all the documents and the evidence you want to use at the hearing even though you have already sent copies to the court and your opponent.

When you arrive at court you will find a list of the days cases on a notice board. Check that your case is listed and inform the usher that you have arrived. The usher will know if your opponent has arrived and if he or she is represented by a solicitor.

Unless you have a relatively long time estimate such as a full day, cases are usually listed in blocks or groups. For example, a number of cases will be listed for 10.00 a.m. and 2.00 p.m. and will be heard in order. This means you are likely to have to spend some time waiting around before the hearing. This gives you an opportunity to check that your opponent has received all the documents you or the court have served on him, and if he has not let him have a look at a copy. The waiting period could also give you an opportunity to settle the dispute if you consider it worthwhile, but beware of accepting an unfavourable settlement because of prehearing nerves. If you do achieve a compromise the judge will most likely approve it at the hearing and issue a consent order.

When it is your turn to be heard the usher will show you into the judge's room. The judge will usually be sitting at the end of a long table. You and your opponent will sit on either side. The judge will not be wearing a wig or gown and should be addressed as "Sir or Madam". Ask the judge if he would prefer the witnesses to wait outside and be called in when required, or if they may sit in on the full hearing. Only the people involved in the case will be present. Evidence is not given on oath unless the district judge directs that it should be.

Because it is the plaintiff who has brought the case to the small claims arbitration and it is the plaintiff who has made allegations or claims against the defendant it is usual for the plaintiff to begin by presenting his case at the hearing. The defendant will then have an opportunity to respond.

HOW TO PRESENT YOUR CASE – THE PLAINTIFF

- As the judge if he or she has all the documents in the case such as the summons, defence, expert's reports and witness statements.

- Take the judge through the list of points you have prepared or the particulars of claim to explain your case. Identify what is admitted by the defendant in the defence. This should give the judge a clear idea of what is at issue and thus what he is being asked to decide.

- If the judge is making notes take account of this and speak fairly slowly.

11 ARBITRATION AND JUDGMENT

- Having given an outline of your case introduce the evidence you have to support it. This may include your own oral evidence, documents and possibly witnesses, although this is not essential.

- You, the judge and your opponent will all have an opportunity to question your witnesses. Try and prepare questions as suggested in chapter ... You will also be able to question your opponent and his witnesses.

- Except when you are questioning witnesses you should address your remarks to the judge. Avoid getting involved in any direct argument with your opponent.

HOW TO PRESENT YOUR CASE – THE DEFENDANT

- You will probably have to wait while the plaintiff presents his claims against you to the judge. This may be very frustrating but do not interrupt or speak over your opponent. You will have an opportunity to put your side of the story later on.

- When the plaintiff is speaking make a note of any important points he makes. For example if there is something you would like to question him about later or a fact that has not emerged previously.

- After the plaintiff has spoken you will have the opportunity to present your defence. Use the notes you have prepared or your defence form to help you as you tell the judge all the important points.

- Try to respond to what the plaintiff has said.

- You will have an opportunity to call your witnesses and question them as well as an opportunity to question your opponent and his witnesses.

- If you have filed a Counterclaim this must be presented as though you were a plaintiff.

Whether you are a plaintiff or a defendant it is in your own best interest to remain calm and courteous throughout the hearing.

FAILURE TO ATTEND

If the plaintiff fails to attend, the judge could decide that there is no case to answer and dismiss the summons. In such a case, the plaintiff could apply for judgment to be set aside if grounds exist. If the defendant fails to attend, the judge could enter judgment for the plaintiff or decide that there is no case to answer and dismiss the summons.

If you find you are going to be unable to attend contact the court immediately to seek an adjournment.

JUDGMENT

If a compromise is not possible, the judge will decide on the evidence whether the plaintiff has proved the case and is entitled to the orders requested. The judge will usually make a decision on the claim and counterclaim (if any) at the hearing. Be careful to write down what the judgment is. The court will prepare the form of judgment and serve it on both sides If it is inaccurate or incorrect, contact the court immediately.

SETTING ASIDE JUDGMENT

It may be possible to have judgment set aside for example. There is more information on setting aside judgments in chapter 13.

It is not possible to appeal.

If judgment is made against you when you are not present, an application can be made within 14 days for judgment to be set aside and the case proceed to another arbitration. Form N244 should be used and reasons must be given.

Now please read the **KEY POINTS** from chapter 11 overleaf.

KEY POINTS

- At the hearing you must present your case, because the Plaintiff has the burden of proof. The judge will be concerned to decide whether the facts you rely on, such as delivery of goods, have been proven, e.g. by producing a signed delivery note.

- The Defendant must answer your case, because the onus of proof will require him to give some explanation. A counter claim must be argued in the same way as a claim.

12 ENFORCING THE JUDGMENT

In this chapter the judgment debtor is referred to as the defendant but judgment debtors can also be plaintiffs who have lost a counterclaim. Once you have obtained judgment on the claim or counterclaim no further action is required so long as the damages are paid. However judgment debtors do not always comply with the court's order to pay a lump sum and may fall into arrears with payments to be made by instalments, in which case you have a number of options and can ask the court for any of the following:

A WARRANT OF EXECUTION (FORM N323)

This gives a bailiff the authority to visit the defendant's home or business and try to collect the money you are owed or to take goods to sell at auction. You can ask the bailiff to recover the whole amount or alternatively you can ask for part of the debt for example one or more instalments, or a minimum of £50. You cannot normally ask for a part warrant if you originally asked for the judgment to be paid in one amount. A fee will be charged and this will be added to the amount you are owed by the defendant. The fee will not be refunded if the bailiff is not able to get anything from the defendant.

To request a warrant of execution fill in form N323 and send it to the court. If you would like confirmation that the warrant has been issued you must also enclose a stamped addressed envelope. The court will send the defendant a notice to let him know that a warrant has been issued and that he must pay what is owed within seven days. If he complies the court will send the moneys on to you. If he does not the bailiff will call at his address within 15 working days of the warrant being issued to collect payment or take goods. The cost of taking and selling such goods will be deducted from the amount they raise when they are sold and then you will be sent your money.

There are limits placed on the type of goods a bailiff may take. He cannot take any items which are necessary for the basic domestic needs of the defendant and his family such as clothing or bedding or any items he requires to do his job or carry on his trade such as tools and vehicles. All property seized must belong to the defendant which means the bailiff cannot take goods which the defendant has on hire purchase, lease or which are rented, or which belong to someone else, such as the defendant's spouse. The bailiff may only take goods likely to fetch money at auction.

The bailiff is not entitled to break into the defendant's house to remove property. He may only enter with permission, however he may be able to break into the defendant's business premises if no–one is living there.

The defendant is entitled to ask that the warrant be suspended, in which case you will have a number of options. You can agree to the suspension of the warrant and accept the defendant's offer of payment, or agree to the suspension and ask that he pay more than the amount he has suggested. This would mean that a court officer would decide how much the defendant can afford to pay. Finally you can say that you do not agree to the suspension of the warrant and a hearing will be arranged.

If you object to the court officers decision about how much the defendant should pay fill in form N244 saying why you object and return it within sixteen days of the date of the postmark shown on the envelope the new order came in. A hearing will be arranged where a district judge will decide what the defendant should pay.

12 ENFORCEMENT

If the warrant is suspended but the defendant still does not pay you can use form N445 to ask the court to reissue the warrant. There is no fee for doing this. If the bailiff was unable to recover any money or goods from the defendant and have further information which means you think he should be able to then you can also reissue the warrant in these circumstances. For example, if you have a new address for the defendant or you can give details of an item the defendant owns and which would be worth selling use form N445 to inform the court.

A warrant lasts for one year. If you have still not received payment near the end of that time you should apply to extend the life of the warrant before the year ends otherwise you will have to ask for another warrant and a fee will be charged.

AN ATTACHMENT OF EARNINGS ORDER (FORM N337)

If the defendant is in employment, he still owes you over £50 and he is behind with his payments you may be able to get an attachment of earnings order against him. This means the court will receive payments direct from the defendants employer either monthly or weekly, depending on how he is paid and then will pass the money on to you.

To request an attachment of earnings order fill in form N337 and send it to the office of the defendant's local court with the fee. If your judgment was obtained in another court you should first write to that original court, explain that you want an attachment of earnings order and ask that the case be transferred. The defendants local court will give you a new case number and you can then send in the request form and fee. Enclose a stamped addressed envelope if you would like confirmation that your request is being dealt with.

The court will tell the defendant to pay the money owed or to fill in a farm giving details of his income, expenditure and employment. A court officer will then decide how much the defendant can afford to pay having made allowance for what he needs to live on. the order will then be sent to the defendant's employer telling him what and when he should pay.

If you are not happy with the court officers decision you can use form N244 to ask for a district judge to decide what the defendant can afford to pay. You must say why you object to the decision and return the form within sixteen days of the date of the postmark shown on the envelope which the attachment of earnings order came in. A hearing will then be arranged.

The defendant is entitled to ask that the order should be suspended and that he should be allowed to make payments directly to you. If the order has been suspended and the defendant still does not pay use form N446 to request reissue of the process so that the court will send the order to his employer. No fee is charged for this.

You cannot obtain an attachment of earnings order against a defendant who is in the army, navy or air force or is a merchant seaman, a firm or a limited company. Nor can you obtain one against a defendant who is self–employed or unemployed. If the defendant is on a very low wage it might not be possible for the court to make such an order.

If the defendant has found new work after a period of unemployment during which the order had lapsed you can use form N446 to ask the court to send the attachment of earnings order to the new employer.

A GARNISHEE ORDER (FORM 349)

If you have obtained a judgment for more than £25 the court can order a person who owes the defendant money or who holds money on their behalf to pay you as much as is needed to cover the balance on your judgment, or if there is not sufficient to pay you as much as they have or owe.

A garnishee order can apply to most debts but is normally used to obtain money from a defendant's bank or building society accounts. You should fill in form N349 giving the name and address of the person who owes the defendant money or the name and branch of the defendant's bank if you know it. The form must then be sworn on oath. This can be done before a court officer at any county court free of charge or before a solicitor who will charge you a small fee.

There will not be a hearing. Your application will be considered by a district judge in private. If he decides to grant the order the court will send a garnishee order nisi to the person who owes or holds the money for the defendant. This person is known as the garnishee. This order will freeze the account. You will be sent a copy and the defendant will also be sent one seven days later. The delay being to stop him taking money from his account to avoid the order.

Before the money is paid to the plaintiff the defendant and the garnishee will have the opportunity to tell the court if there are any good reasons why the garnishee order nisi should not be made absolute. For example the money really belongs to someone else or the account is overdrawn. If they do not have a reason the court will make a garnishee order absolute which will mean the garnishee has to pay the money to the plaintiff.

The order only freezes the money which was held on the date when the bank or person received the order. It does not cover money paid in later. Therefore it is a good idea to try and have it served when they are likely to have as much money as possible for example at the beginning of the month if that is when their salary is paid.

A CHARGING ORDER AND ORDER FOR SALE

If the defendant does not have identifiable income or money for you to claim but does own property such as a house (either freehold or leasehold) or something such as bonds, stocks and shares, you can obtain a charging order over this property. The effect would be that you would have a right to part of the value of the property and when it is sold you will receive your money.

To obtain a charging order you must prove that the debtor owns the property. In the case of land this means obtaining "Office Copy Entries" from HM Land Registry for which you will need to complete a "Public Index Map" search to find out the title number of the land.

Unlike the other types of enforcement proceedings there is no application form for a charging order. You must write and swear an affidavit saying that the defendant owes you money and giving the details. You should also say that the debt is a result of a judgment and give the date, case number and details of the judgment. State what the outstanding balance of the debt is, then send the affidavit to the court with the document from the land registry and the fee.

Once you have a charging order you can ask the court to order the defendant to sell his property to pay the debt. This is a separate procedure and you will have to issue fresh proceedings (make an originating application) and pay another fee. In practice it is difficult to obtain such an order. The court is unlikely to order the sale of a valuable property or family home to pay a small debt. You are likely to find that the defendant's home is jointly owned by his or her spouse. even if they are not registered as a legal owner a husband or wife can have rights over a house known as a "beneficial interest" which could stop you obtaining an order for sale. Furthermore the property is likely to be mortgaged and the mortgagee may well oppose the sale.

You should take advice before applying for a charging order and especially before applying for an order for sale as these procedures can be complicated and costly.

ORAL EXAMINATION (FORM N316)

This is not a method of enforcement but is a means of finding out information about the defendant to enable you to decide if he is able to pay you and which method of enforcement would be most appropriate. You can request an oral examination by filling in form N316 and sending it to the defendant's local court with the fee. If you obtained your judgment in a different court you must first write to that original court asking for the case to be transferred, and then send your form and fee in once this has been done.

If the defendant is a company you can request an oral examination of one of the directors. You can find out who the directors are by telephoning Companies House on 01222 380801. the case should be transferred to the court nearest the director's home or business address rather than the one nearest to the company's registered office.

The court will send the defendant a form telling him when to attend court and instructing him to bring any documents concerning his finances. The court may also send out a questionnaire for the defendant to complete prior to the hearing.

You will be notified of when the examination is to take place. Check whether you are required to attend. If you cannot but you have specific questions which you would like the defendant to be asked write to the court and ask that they be included in the examination. You will receive a copy of the defendant's answers after the examination.

If the defendant fails to attend the examination will normally be adjourned and rescheduled for a new date. If this happens you may have to pay the defendant's reasonable travelling expenses to the attend on the new date, known as "conduct money". The defendant is entitled to ask you for this at any time up to seven days before the date fixed for the adjourned examination.

It is important that you write to the court just prior to the examination (no more than four days beforehand) to let them know that you have paid a reasonable amount for travelling expenses or that the defendant has not asked you for conduct money. If you have paid his expenses and the defendant fails to attend that amount will be added to what he owes you.

An order to attend an adjourned oral examination must be served personally by a bailiff. If the defendant fails to attend the judge can issue a warrant for his arrest provided that he is satisfied the defendant knew of the examination. The bailiff will then arrest the defendant and bring him to the court to be examined. The court will send you a copy of his answers.

APPOINTMENT OF A RECEIVER

Receivership orders are made where it is not impossible to use any of the other legal methods of enforcement. The order will authorise the receiver to receive money, rent and profits which the judgment debtor is entitled to because of his interest in specified property. When deciding whether or not to appoint a receiver the court will take into account the amount that is owed, the amount that is likely to be obtained by a receiver and the probable costs of the appointment. It is not a usual course of action for recovering debts arising out of small claims.

An application for the appointment of a receiver must be supported by two affidavits. One stating the grounds for the order and giving details of the debt and property to be administered. The second must be sworn by an independent person who has known the receiver for at least five years and can swer that he is fit to be appointed.

Bankruptcy Proceedings

Non payment of the debt could give you grounds to issue a bankruptcy petition against the defendant. The debt must exceed £750, it must be unsecured and the debtor must either be unable to pay or have no reasonable prospect of being able to pay.

Plaintiff's Obligations

If you have begun any of the enforcement proceedings and you receive full or partial payment from the defendant you must tell the court immediately.

KEY POINTS

- Obtaining judgment may not be the end of the matter you may need to take further proceedings to enforce your rights.

- Choose the most appropriate method of enforcement and remember that you must convince a Judge that the order should be made.

- If the debtor has no assets enforcement procedures will not be successful.

12 ENFORCEMENT

Request for Oral Examination

1. Plaintiff's name and address

2. Name and address for service and payment (if different from above) Ref/Tel No.

3. Defendant's name and address

4. Name and address of person to be orally examined (if different from Box 3)

5. Judgment details

Court where judgment/order made if not court of issue

6. Outstanding debt

Balance of debt and any interest*/damages at date of this request

Issue fee

AMOUNT NOW DUE

Unsatisfied warrant costs

In the

County Court

Case Number

I apply for an order that the above defendant (the officer of the defendant company named in Box 4) attend and be orally examined as to his (the defendant company's) financial circumstances and produce at the examination any relevant books or documents

I certify that the balance now due is as shown

Signed

Plaintiff (Plaintiff's solicitor)

Dated

IMPORTANT
You must inform the court immediately of any payments you receive after you have sent this request to the court

N316 Request for oral examination (Order 25, rule 3(1A))

A STRAIGHTFORWARD GUIDE TO SMALL CLAIMS

Request for Attachment of Earnings Order

to be completed and signed by the plaintiff or his solicitor and sent to the court with the appropriate fee

1 Plaintiff's name and address

In the

County Court

Case Number

2 Name and address for service and payment (if different from above)
Ref/Tel No.

for court use only

A/E application no.

Issue date:

Hearing date:

on

at   o'clock

at (address)

3 Defendant's name and address

4 Judgment details

Date of judgment/order

Court where judgment/order made if not court of issue

5 Outstanding debt

Balance due at date of this request

Issue fee

AMOUNT NOW DUE

Unsatisfied warrant costs

I apply for an attachment of earnings order

I certify that the whole or part of any instalments due under the judgment or order have not been paid and the balance now due is as shown

Signed

Plaintiff (Plaintiff's solicitor)

Dated

6 Employment Details *(please give as much information as you can)*

Employer's name and address

Defendant's place of work (if different from employer's address)

The defendant is employed as

Works No/Pay Ref.

Please proceed with this application in my absence *(delete if for maintenance or otherwise appropriate)*

IMPORTANT
You must inform the court immediately of any payments you receive after you have sent this request to the court

13 IF JUDGMENT HAS BEEN ENTERED AGAINST YOU

If you were unsuccessful in your case and an order has been made that you should pay your opponent you should send the payments directly to him or his representative. The name and address for payment will be shown on the court forms. You should not send payments to the court. The judgment order will tell you when to pay and if it should be by instalments. It is important that you pay on time because if you are late, even by one day, the plaintiff will be able to ask the court to take the steps outlined in the previous chapter and you are likely to have to pay the costs of such action. Always allow plenty of time for the payment to arrive. The courts recommend you allow at least four clear working days before it is due. You should pay by cheque or postal order or some other method which gives you proof you have paid. Do not send cash. You should keep a record of all the payments you make and when you send them enclose your name, address, case number and plaintiff's reference with your payment.

SETTING THE JUDGMENT ASIDE

If you did not receive the summons and a judgment in default has been entered against you you can ask for the judgment to be set aside, which means cancelled by filling in form N244. No fee is charged. You can only ask for the judgment to be set aside on those grounds if you think that you do not have the money.

The court will arrange a hearing at which the district judge will decide whether or not to cancel the judgment. If the judgment was not made in your local court you should have the case transferred there before a hearing is arranged.

Judgments can also be set aside if there has been misconduct by the arbitrator or he made an error of law. Misconduct can include misuse of information and in some circumstances rejection of evidence or the reception of evidence in the absence of the parties.

VARYING THE ORDER

If you have been ordered to pay the whole judgment debt as one lump sum or by instalments which are too large you can use form N245 to ask the court to vary the order and reduce the payments. The plaintiff will be asked if he will agree to accept what you are offering to pay. If he will not the court will decide want you should pay. If you do not accept their decision you should write within sixteen days of the date of the postmark on the varied order giving your reasons and asking that the matter should be reconsidered. A hearing with a district judge will be arranged at your local court where the matter will be decided.

INABILITY TO PAY

If you have no income and cannot pay anything towards the debt at the moment ask the court for a stay of judgment on form N244. A hearing with a district judge will be arranged.

13 IF JUDGMENT HAS BEEN ENTERED AGAINST YOU

SUSPENSION OF WARRANTS AND ORDERS

When the plaintiff tries to recover money using one of the enforcement procedures outlined in the previous chapter you will have the opportunity to apply for the warrant or order to be suspended.

THE REGISTER OF COUNTY COURT JUDGMENTS

The judgment will be entered on the County Court Judgments Register and will remain there for six years. This may make it difficult for you to obtain credit, a mortgage or goods on hire purchase. Banks, building societies and credit companies search the Register. The Office of Fair Trading produces a booklet called "No Credit" explaining what you can do if you are refused credit. You can telephone them on 0181 398 3405 to ask for a copy.

If you pay the full amount you owe within one month of the judgment date, you can ask the court to take your name off the register. You will have to pay a fee of £3 and give the court proof that you have paid, for example a letter from the plaintiff. The court will cancel your entry on the register and give you a certificate of satisfaction which proves you paid within one month.

If you do not pay within one month you can ask the court to mark the register "satisfied" when you have paid the full amount which you owe. This will mean that anyone who searches the register will know you have paid the debt and when your last payment was made. You will receive a certificate of satisfaction but the entry will remain on the register for six years. To obtain this send the fee of £3 and proof of payment.

ADMINISTRATION ORDERS

If you have at least two outstanding debts and at least one of them is a result of a judgment you can apply to the court for an administration order using form N92. To be eligible the total sum of your debts must not be more than £5,000. The effect of an arbitration order would be that the court would help you to administer your finances and in the meantime none of your creditors would be able to take enforcement action or to make you bankrupt without referring to the court first.

If an administration order is made instead of paying for creditors directly you would make monthly payments to the court which would then divide the money between your creditors. The court will decide how much you have to pay after considering the information you give about your income and expenditure in your application form. You can suggest a rate at which you could pay but be realistic. Make sure it is an amount you really can afford and that you have allowed yourself enough for your basic needs.

If you have a job the court might make an order that your employer should deduct money from your earnings and send it straight to them. If you do not want this to happen indicate on your application form that you do not want an attachment of earnings order.

Fill in the form but do not sign it then take it to your local county court where you will be asked to swear on oath that the information you have given in your application is true and to sign the form in front of a court officer. If you have any documents which support your statements about your income and expenditure take them with you, for example bills and receipts.

When the court has fixed a rate of payment you and your creditors will be given 16 days in which to object. If anyone does object a hearing will be arranged.

13 IF JUDGMENT HAS BEEN ENTERED AGAINST YOU

If you have trouble paying the amount ordered contact the court immediately. If you fail to pay the court has the power to issue a warrant of execution, to make an attachment of earnings order or to revoke the administration order in which case your creditors can enforce their rights themselves. If you incur more debts after the order has been made these can only be added with the agreement of the court.

The administration order will be entered on the register of county court judgments which will mean you are likely to find it difficult to obtain credit until your debts are paid.

A COMPOSITION ORDER

When an administration order has been made the court may, in some circumstances, make an order that you do not have to pay the full amount which you owe. It reduces proportionately the amount owed to your various creditors.

INDIVIDUAL VOLUNTARY ARRANGEMENTS

You can suggest a Voluntary Arrangement which is a legally binding contract between you and your unsecured creditors. You can make a proposal for payment but it only becomes binding once the creditors have accepted it. The creditors do not have to receive the full amount due but it must be more than they would receive under your bankruptcy.

You can ask for an interim order to stay all proceedings while the creditors consider the proposal but you will need an insolvency practitioner to make the application for you which will be expensive.

BANKRUPTCY

An individual can file his own petition to make himself bankrupt on a voluntary basis. There is a fee of £275 for this and you will need to produce a statement of affairs disclosing all assets and liabilities, and fill in a form for the court. When a debtor owes under £20,000 and is made bankrupt voluntarily rather than at the request of his creditors he may be an undischarged bankrupt for only two years rather than the usual three. Bankruptcy has serious consequences and you would be ill-advised to make such an application without seeking advice.

Now read the **KEY POINTS** of chapter 13.

13 IF JUDGMENT HAS BEEN ENTERED AGAINST YOU

KEY POINTS

- Keep a record of all payments made to the Plaintiff.

- You can ask the Court to set the judgment aside or vary the order or to grant a stay of judgment if you cannot pay.

- You can apply to have the warrant or order suspended.

- A judgment against you will be entered on the County Court Judgment Register. If you pay the full amount within one month you can ask for your name to be removed.

GLOSSARY OF IMPORTANT TERMS

Action — The name given to legal proceedings

Attachment of Earnings — Enforcement of a judgement debt by deducting payments from salary or earnings

Bailiff — The court officer who enforces warrents of execution. Also used to serve documents

Burden of Proof — The term which means that the plaintiff must prove his case. A case made by way of counterclaim

Charging Order — Enforcement of a judgement by a mortgage over property belonging to the debtor

Chief Clerk — The head administrator of the court to whom all letters should be addressed

Case reference — The number given to each case which must be quoted on all

Counterclaim — A separate claim made by the defendant against the plaintiff

County Court	The civil court which conducts arbitrations of small claims
Damages	The legal term for the compensation the court orders the successful party to pay the unsuccessful party
Default summons	A type of summons or action which allows the plaintiff judgement without a hearing if the defendant does not file a defence
Defendant	The party who is sued
Defence	The rejection of a claim filed by the defendant
Directions	Court orders informing the parties of any preliminary action to take before the arbitration
District Judge	The judge who will act as arbiter at the arbitration of the small claim
Evidence	The process by which the facts of a case are established, for the benefit of the judge. Evidence may be oral or documentary

GLOSSARY

Expert	A person who has an expertise which is recognised by the court
Expert evidence	Evidence given by an expert to support a case, consisting of an expert report and oral evidence
Form of Admission	The court form used by the defendant to admit or partially admit a claim, and to offer payment by instalments
Form of Defence	The form used by the defendant to counterclaim file a defence or counterclaim
Garnishee Order	An enforcement order requiring a creditor of the judgement debtor to pay monies into court on account of the debt to the successful party
Judgement	The court's determination of a case ordering the parties to take certain action, usually a payment of money
Litigant	The plaintiff or defendant
Liquidated Sum	A fixed claim as opposed to an unknown claim

Onus of Proof	The obligation to answer or rebut allegations made by the other side
Open letter	A letter offering a settlement which is intended to be binding, compared to a "without prejudice" letter or offer
Oral Examination	An examination of a debtor on oath in court whereby the successful party asks questions with a view to choosing a suitable method of enforcement
Order for Sale	An order enforcing a charging order and is rare
Plaintiff	The party who starts an action
Plaint Note	The form received by the Plaintiff when a summons is issued
Pre-Trial Review	A pre-hearing ordered by the district judge, unusual in small claims
Prove	To give evidence which "on the balance of probabilities" shows that an argument is correct

GLOSSARY

Request for Judgement	The form filed by the plaintiff when the summons is ignored
Service	Delivering court documents to the other side
Small Claim	A monetary claim of less than £1,000
Unliquidated Sum	A claim for damages to be assessed, where the exact amount is not known
Warrant of Execution	Enforcement whereby the court bailiff seizes goods belonging to the debtor for sale
Without prejudice	An offer which is not binding

APPENDIX 1

Example 1

PARTICULARS OF CLAIM

1. The Defendants are and were at all material times in the business of selling cleaning products.

2. On the 7th February 1996 the Defendants in the course of the said business contracted with the Plaintiff and sold 4 bottles of "miracle clean" detergent at a price of £99.

3. At the time of the said contract the Plaintiff told the Defendants that the said detergent would be used for the purpose of cleaning the curtains and carpets at his flat at 10, Gillespie Drive, Warwickshire.

4. It was an implied term of the said contract that the said detergent should be :

reasonably fit
a) reasonably fit for the said purpose

b) of satisfactory quality.

5. On the 10th February the Plaintiff used the said detergent to clean curtains and carpets at his flat.

6. In breach of the said implied terms the said detergent was not fit for the required purpose and was not of satisfactory quality in that it damaged the plaintiff's curtains and carpets beyond repair. The said curtains and carpets lost their colour and developed large holes.

7. By reason of the matters aforesaid the Plaintiff has suffered loss and damage.

PARTICULARS OF DAMAGE

1) Value of carpets	£1,000
2) Cost of removing the old carpets and fitting new carpets	£ 200
3) Value of curtains	£ 300
	£1,500

AND the plaintiff claims
1) Damages
2) Interest
3) Costs

DEFENCE AND COUNTERCLAIM

---

1. Paragraphs 1, 2, 3 and 4 of the Particulars of Claim are admitted.

2. Paragraph 5 is not admitted.

3. It is denied that the Defendants were in breach of the said implied terms as alleged in paragraph 6 of the Particulars of Claim or at all. In particular it is denied that the damage was caused by the said detergent. Alternatively if the damage was caused by the said

detergent it is averred that this was a result of the Plaintiff's failure to follow the instructions for use printed on the bottles.

4. No admission is made as to the alleged or any loss and damage or the amount thereof. It is denied that any loss and damage suffered by the Plaintiff was caused by any breach of contract by the Defendants.

5. If contrary to their Defence the Defendants are held liable to the Plaintiff they will seek to set off so much of the sum counterclaimed herein as may extinguish or diminish such liability.

COUNTERCLAIM

6. Paragraph 1 hereof is repeated.

7. On the 14th February 1996 the Defendants by their invoice No. 6966 demanded from the Plaintiff the sum of £99 pursuant to the said contract. Despite frequent requests, oral and written, for payment the Plaintiff has not paid the Defendant the said sum or any part thereof.

AND the Defendants claim

1) £99
2) Interest

APPENDIX 1

Example 2

PARTICULARS OF CLAIM
---

1. On 13th April 1995 at about 10 pm the Plaintiff was walking across Parsons Road when the Defendant drove his Range Rover car registration number .... from Widney Avenue onto Parsons Road, hit the Plaintiff and knocked him down.

2. The accident was caused by the negligence of the Defendant.

PARTICULARS OF NEGLIGENCE

a) The Defendant was negligent in that he drove too fast in all the circumstances

b) failed to keep any, or any proper look-out

c) failed to stop, slow down, steer or otherwise control his car so as to avoid hitting the Plaintiff

3. As a result of the said accident the Plaintiff suffered pain, injury, loss and damage.

PARTICULARS OF INJURY

a) sprained left wrist

b) bruises

c) pain and shock

Further particulars of the Plaintiff's injuries are set out in the medical report served herewith.

PARTICULARS OF SPECIAL DAMAGE

a) Broken wrist watch £ 60

b) Loss of earnings £100

AND the Plaintiff claims

1) Damages
2) Interest
3) Costs

DEFENCE

---

1. Paragraph 1 is admitted.

2. The Defendant denies that he was negligent as alleged or at all or that the said accident was caused by any negligence on his part.

3. The said accident was caused solely by or contributed to by the negligence of the Plaintiff

PARTICULARS OF NEGLIGENCE

a) Failing to look or look properly before steppingout

b) Failing to observe the Defendant's car

c) Failing to stop, step aside or take any other action to avoid being struck by the Defendant's car

4. No admission is made as to the alleged or any pain, injury, loss or damage or as to the amount thereof.

APPENDIX 2

ORDER 19

REFERENCE TO ARBITRATION OR FOR INQUIRY AND REPORT OR TO EUROPEAN COURT

1 Interpretation and Application

In this Part of this Order, unless the context otherwise requires -

lay representative means a person exercising a right of audience by virtue of an order made under section 11 of the Courts and Legal Services Act 1990 (representation in county courts),

reference means the reference of proceedings to arbitration under section 64 of the Act,

order means an order referring proceedings to arbitration under that section and

outside arbitrator means an arbitrator other than the judge or district judge.

2 In this Part of this Order

(a) Rules 3 and 4 apply only to small claims automatically referred to arbitration under rule 3, and

(b) Rules 5 to 10 apply to all arbitrations.

3 Automatic Reference of Small Claims

(1) Any proceedings in which the sum claimed or amount involved does not exceed £1,000 (leaving out of account the sum claimed or amount involved in any counterclaim) shall stand referred for arbitration by the district judge upon the receipt by the court of a defence to the claim.

(2) Where any proceedings are referred for arbitration by the district judge under paragraph (1), he may, after considering the defence and whether on the application of any party of his own

motion, order trial in court if he is satisfied -

(a) that a difficult question of law or a question of fact of exceptional complexity is involved; or

(b) that fraud is alleged against a party; or

(c) that the parties are agreed that the dispute should be tried in court; or

(d) that it would be unreasonable for the claim to proceed to arbitration having regard to its subject matter, the size of any counterclaim, the circumstances of the parties or the interests of any other person likely to be affected by the award.

(3) Where the district judge is minded to order trial in court of his own motion -

(a) the proper officer shall notify the parties in writing specifying on which of the grounds mentioned in paragraph (2) the district judge is minded to order trial in court;

(b) within 14 days after service of the proper officer's notice on him, a party may give written notice stating his reasons for objecting to the making of the order;

(c) if in any notice under sub-paragraph (b) a party so requests, the proper officer shall fix a day for a hearing at which the district judge -

(i) shall decide whether to order trial in court, and

(ii) may give directions regarding the steps to be taken before or at any subsequent hearing as if he were conducting a preliminary appointment or, as the case may be, a pre-trial review; and, in the absence of any request under sub-paragraph (c), the district judge may, in the absence of the parties, order trial in court.

(4) For the purposes of paragraph (1), 'a defence to the claim' includes a document admitting liability for the claim but disputing or not admitting the amount claimed.

4   Restriction on Allowance of Costs in Small Claims

(1) In this rule, 'costs' means -

(a) solicitors' charges,

(b) sums allowed to a litigant in person pursuant to Order 38, rule 17,

(c) a fee or reward charged by a lay representative for acting on behalf of a party in the proceedings.

(2) No costs shall be allowed as between party and party in respect of any proceedings referred to arbitration under rule 3, except -

(a)   the costs which were stated on the summons or which would have been stated on the summons if the claim had been for a liquidated sum;

(b)   the costs of enforcing the award, and

(c)   such further costs as the district judge may direct where there has been unreasonable conduct on the part of the opposite party in relation to the proceedings or the claim therein.

(3)   Nothing in paragraph (2) shall be taken as precluding the award of the following allowances -

(a)   any expenses which have been reasonably incurred by a party or a witness in travelling to and from the hearing or in staying away from home;

(b)   a sum not exceeding £29.00 in respect of a party's or a witness's loss of earnings when attending a hearing;

(c)   a sum not exceeding £112.50 in respect of the fees of an expert.

(4) Where trial in court is ordered, paragraph (2) shall not apply to costs incurred after the date of the order.

(5) Where costs are directed under paragraph (2)(c), those costs shall not be, those costs shall not be taxed and the amount to be allowed shall be specified by the arbitrator or the district judge.

5 The Arbitrator

(1) Unless the court otherwise orders, the district judge shall be the arbitrator.

(2) An order shall not be made referring proceedings to the Circuit judge except by or with the leave of the judge.

(3) An order shall not be made referring proceedings to an outside arbitrator except with the consent of the parties.

(4) Where proceedings are referred to an outside arbitrator, the order shall be served on the arbitrator as well as on the parties, but it shall not, unless the court directs, be served on anyone until each party has paid into court such sum as the district judge may determine in respect of the arbitrator's remuneration.

6 Preparation for the Hearing

(1) Paragraph (2) of this rule shall apply unless the district judge -

(a) is minded to order trial in court under rule 3 (3) or

(b) decides that a preliminary appointment should be held.

(2) Upon the reference to arbitration the district judge shall consider the documents filed and give an estimate of the time allowed for the hearing and the proper officer shall -

(a) give the parties not less than 21 days' notice of the day fixed for the hearing; and

(b) issue directions under paragraph (3) in the appropriate form regarding the steps to be taken before or at any subsequent hearing.

(3) Where proceedings stand referred to arbitration, the following directions shall take effect -

(a) each party shall not less than 14 days before the date fixed for the hearing send to every other party copies of all documents which are in his possession and on which that party intends to rely at the hearing;

(b) each party shall not less than 7 days before the date fixed for the hearing send to the court and to every other party a copy of any expert report on which that party intends to rely at the hearing and a list of the witnesses whom he intends to call at the hearing.

(4) A preliminary appointment shall only be held -

(a) where directions under paragraph (3) are not sufficient and special directions can only be given in the presence of the parties, or

(b) to enable the district judge to dispose of the case where the claim is ill-founded or there is no reasonable defence. In deciding whether to hold a preliminary appointment, the district judge shall have regard to the desirability of minimising the number of court attendances by the parties.

(5) Where the district judge decides to hold a preliminary appointment, the proper officer shall fix a date for the appointment and give to the plaintiff and the defendant not less than 8 days' notice of the day so fixed.

(6) On the preliminary appointment the district judge shall have the same powers as he has under Order 17 on a pre-trial review and he shall -

(a) give an estimate of the time to be allowed for the hearing (unless the parties consent to his deciding the dispute on the statements and documents submitted to him); and

(b) whether of his own motion or at the request of a party, give such additional directions regarding the steps to be taken before and at the hearing as may appear to him to be necessary or desirable. Dirrections given under sub-paragraph (b) may include (but shall not be limited to) a requirement that a party should clarify or, as the case may be, his defence.

(7) After the preliminary appointment, the proper officer shall -

(a) give the parties not less than 21 days' notice of the

day fixed for the hearing; and

(b) issue directions under paragraph (3) in the appropriate form regarding he steps to be taken before or at the hearing together with any additional directions given pursuant to paragraph (6)(b).

(8) The district judge may from time to time whether on application or of his own motion amend or add to any directions issued if he thinks it necessary to do so in the circumstances of the case.

(9) The following provisions of these rules shall not apply where proceedings stand referred to arbitration:

(a) Order 6, rule 7 (further particulars),

(b) Order 9, rule 11 (particulars of defence),

(c) Order 14, rules 1 (2), 3 to 5 5A and 11 (discovery and interrogatories), and

(d) Order 20, rules 2 and 3 (notices to admit facts and documents),

(e) Order 20, rule 12A (exchange of witness statements). Order 11, rules 1, 1A, 3 to 5, 7, 8 and 10 (payments into court) and Order 13, rule 1 (8) (a) (security for costs) shall not apply where proceedings stand referred to arbitration under rule 3.

(10) If it appears to the court at any time after a reference has been made (whether by order or otherwise) that there are any other matters within the jurisdiction of the court in dispute between the parties, the court may order them also to be referred to arbitration.

7 Conduct of Hearing

(1) Any proceedings referred to arbitration shall be dealt with in accordance with the following paragraphs of this rule unless the arbitrator otherwise orders.

(2) The hearing may be held at the court house, at the court office or at any other place convenient to the parties.

(3) The hearing shall be informal and the strict rules of evidence shall not apply; unless the arbitrator orders otherwise, the hearing shall be held in private and evidence shall not be taken on oath.

(4) At the hearing the arbitrator may adopt any method of procedure which he may consider to be fair and which gives to each party an equal opportunity to have his case presented; having considered the circumstances of the parties and whether (or to what extent) they are represented, the arbitrator -

> (a) may assist a party by putting questions to the witnesses and the other party; and
>
> (b) should explain any legal terms or expressions which are used.

(5) If any party does not appear at the arbitration, the arbitrator may, after taking into account any pleadings or other documents filed, make an award on hearing any other party to the proceedings who may be present.

(6) With the consent of the parties and at any time before giving his decision, the district judge may consult any expert or call for an expert report on any matter in dispute or invite an expert to attend the hearing as assessor.

(7) The arbitrator may require the production of any document or thing and may inspect any property or thing concerning which any question may arise.

(8) The arbitrator shall inform the parties of his award and give reasons for it to any party who may be present at the hearing.

8   Setting Awards Aside

(1) Where proceedings are referred to arbitration, the award of the arbitrator shall be final and may only be set aside pursuant to paragraph (2) or on the ground that there has been misconduct by the arbitrator or that the arbitrator made an error of law.

(2) Where an award has been given in the absence of a party, the arbitrator shall have power, on that party's application, to set the award aside and to order a fresh hearing as if the award were a judgement and the application were made pursuant to Order 37, rule 2.

(3) An application by a party to set aside an award by a district judge or an outside arbitrator on the ground mentioned in paragraph (1) shall be made on notice and the notice shall be served within 14 days after the day on which the award was entered as the judgement of the court.

(4) An application under paragraph (3) shall, giving sufficient particulars, set out the misconduct or error of law relied upon.

(5) Order 37, rule 1 (rehearing of proceedings tried without a jury) shall not apply to proceedings referred to arbitration.

9 Mode of Voluntary Reference

(1) Except as provided by rule 3, a reference shall be made only on the application a party to the proceedings sought to be referred.

(2) Unless the court otherwise directs, an application by a party to any proceedings or a reference may be made -

> (a) in the case of a plaintiff, by request incorporated in his particulars of claim;

> (b) in the case of a defendant, by request incorporated in any defence or counterclaim of his;

> (c) in any case, on notice under Order 13, rule.

(3) Where an application for a reference is made under paragraph (1) and the proceedings are not referred to arbitration under rule 3, the following provisions shall apply:

> (a) Subject to rule 5 (2) and sub-paragraphs (b) and (c) below, an order may be made by the district judge.

> (b) If the court is satisfied that an allegation of fraud against a party is in issue in the proceedings, an order shall not be made except with the consent of that party.

> (c) Where the district judge is minded to grant an application under paragraph (1), the proper officer shall notify the parties in writing accordingly and within 14 days after service of the proper officer's notice on him, a party may give written notice stating his reasons for objecting to the reference; if in any such notice a party so requests,

the proper officer shall fix a day for a hearing at which the district judge shall decide whether to grant the application and, in the absence of any such request, the district judge may consider the application in the absence of the parties.

10 Costs

Subject to rule 4, the costs of the action up to and including the entry of judgement shall be in the discretion of the arbitrator to be exercised in the same manner as the discretion of the court under the provisions of the County Court Rules.